workbook
Innovations

a course in natural English

Hugh Dellar and Andrew Walkley

NATIONAL GEOGRAPHIC LEARNING | CENGAGE Learning

Australia • Brazil • Japan • Korea • Mexico • Singapore • Spain • United Kingdom • United States

**Innovations: a course in natural English,
Advanced Workbook**
Hugh Dellar and Andrew Walkley

Publisher: Christopher Wenger

Series Editor: Jimmie Hill

Director of Product Development: Anita Raducanu

Director of Product Marketing: Amy Mabley

Project Manager: Howard Middle / HM ELT Services

Intl. Marketing Manager: Ian Martin

Editor: Liz Driscoll

Production Management: Process ELT
    (www.process-elt.com)

Sr. Print Buyer: Mary Beth Hennebury

Associate Marketing Manager: Laura Needham

Illustrator: Nick Dimitriadis

Photo Researcher: Process ELT

Cover/Text Designer: Studio Image & Photographic Art
    (www.studio-image.com)

Photo Credits
Photos on pages 17 and 66 from Photos.com.

ISBN: 978-1-4130-2850-8

National Geographic Learning
Cheriton House
North Way
Andover
Hampshire
SP10 5BE
United Kingdom

Cengage Learning is a leading provider of customized learning solutions with office locations around the globe, including Singapore, the United Kingdom, Australia, Mexico, Brazil and Japan. Locate your local office at: **international.cengage.com/region**

Cengage Learning products are represented in Canada by Nelson Education, Ltd.

Visit National Geographic Learning online at **ngl.cengage.com**

Visit our corporate website at **www.cengage.com**

Printed in China by RR Donnelley
6 7 8 9 10 – 17 16 15 14 13

To the student

Studying on your own outside class is just as important as the work you do in class with your teacher. You can make the learning process faster and more efficient if you study at home. Obviously, learning is not something that happens immediately or necessarily when you want it to happen. Learning a language properly is a long, slow process, and at this level it's easy to get disheartened and feel you are no longer making progress. This Workbook aims to combat such feelings and to help you reach a level of real proficiency.

This book is written with two main goals in mind. Firstly, it helps you remember the language you have studied in class. If you really want to be able to use the language you study, you need to meet it quite a few times – and this book will make sure that happens. It gives you more opportunities to practise grammar, it helps to check your understanding of how to use new vocabulary in typical, everyday ways, and it helps you develop your written English too. Secondly, this Workbook expands upon many different specific areas and presents plenty of new, additional language for you to work on.

Here is some general advice for how to get the most out of this book:

- Do a little every day rather than a lot once a week.
- Try to do the exercises in the book without using the Answer Key, but don't worry if you need to use the Answer Key when you have a problem.
- Look back at earlier units in the book after you have finished them. It is important to make sure you remember what you have already studied. Sometimes, just re-reading exercises you did a few weeks before can help you to remember things.
- In some exercises there may be more than one correct answer. This is perfectly normal. There is often more than one way of saying something.

1 Describing people

1 Describing what people are like

Complete the sentences with the pairs of words in the box.

egomaniac + power	push + intimidating
fancies + leave	slob + lifts
know-all + knows	tight-fisted + recycles
laid-back + loses	whinger + petty

1. He's so .... ! He even .... his Christmas cards to try and save money!

2. He's very .... He never .... his temper.

3. He's such a .... ! He just thinks he .... everything about everything.

4. He's an .... ! Honestly, he's .... mad!

5. I think he .... himself as a bit of a ladies' man, a bit of a Casanova. Love them and .... them!

6. He's such a .... ! He's forever going on about his .... little problems!

7. Her boyfriend is such a .... ! He never .... a finger round the house.

8. I think he's a bit of a bully, to be honest. He likes to .... people around. He can be quite ....

2 Word building: opposites

Make the opposites of these adjectives by adding the prefixes in the box.

dis	im	in	un

1. caring ....caring
2. respectful ....respectful
3. inclined ....inclined
4. sociable ....sociable
5. articulate ....articulate
6. likeable ....likeable
7. patient ....patient
8. competent ....competent
9. cooperative ....cooperative
10. decisive ....decisive

3 Common adjectives

Complete the sentences with adjectives from Exercise 2. Can you complete them without looking back?

1. Have you heard the way he talks to his girlfriend? He treats her like dirt. He's so dis......................... to her!

2. Why doesn't the boss just get rid of him? The guy's completely in......................... . He doesn't know what he's doing!

3. I've tried talking to the landlord about it, but he's being really un......................... . He just seems unwilling to help.

4. He's got this painfully slow way of expressing himself. I suppose you could say he's quite in......................... .

5. She strikes me as being a very un......................... person. She seems not to worry about other people's feelings at all.

6. They seem quite dis......................... to offer me a place on the course.

7. I can't stand the guy. I think he's just a thoroughly dis......................... piece of work!

8. You're so in......................... ! Just make up your mind which one you want so we can get out of here and go home.

9. Don't be so un......................... . It'll be nice to go out and meet a few new people for a change.

10. He's useless to go shopping with. He just gets really im......................... and keeps asking me if I'm ready to leave yet.

Now complete these expressions with ONE word from the sentences above.

a. He treats her like ....
b. The boss should just get .... of him.
c. It's .... slow.
d. He .... me as being a bit odd.
e. She's .... dislikeable.
f. He's a nasty piece of .... !

4 Modifying nouns and adjectives

Choose the correct words.

1. He's *quite / an absolute* macho.

2. She's *so / such a* hypocrite.

3. To be honest, he's *not that / not really* bright.

4. He's *so / such a* smug it drives me mad!

5. She's *a bit / a bit of a* weirdo.

6. You're *so / such a* scrounger! Buy your own coffee!

7. She's *really / a real* bore. Honestly, she's deadly dull!

8. Don't get me wrong. I do like him, but he's *not quite that / not really all that* easy to talk to.

5 Idioms: parts of the body

Complete the sentences with the words in the box.

back	eyes	head	shoulder
chest	face	neck	

1. I've already got a lot on my plate, and my boss is constantly breathing down my .... to get things finished and do more. It's really annoying.

2. I wouldn't trust her as far as I could throw her. I've heard her talking behind your .... a couple of times.

3. We just got the giggles and I was desperately trying to keep a straight .... , which just made things worse.

4. She was already in a bad mood, but she nearly bit my .... off when I asked what time dinner was.

5. A: Thanks for listening to all my problems. I really needed to get things off my ....

   B: Don't worry. If you ever need a .... to cry on or you just want to vent your frustrations, I'm here.

6. A: I really don't like the way he .... you up and down while he's talking to you.

   B: I know. He gives me the creeps.

Language note

If you've got *a lot on your plate*, you have lots of work to do.

If you *get the giggles*, you laugh uncontrollably, usually about something silly.

If you *vent your frustrations* or *your anger*, you express your feelings in a strong way.

6 Keyword: *stick*

Find 16 sentences with the word *stick*. Mark the end of each sentence using /. Translate the sentences into your own language.

peopleheretendtosticktogetherintimesoftroubleIdidn't
managetosticktothedietintheendifyoustickatitI'msureyou'll
getbetterIgotstucknexttothisnutteronthebusweshouldstick
someofthesephotosinanalbumitbrokebutImanagedtostickit
backtogetherwithsellotapeshe'sstuckinadead-endjobjuststick
yourbagsinthecornerforthemomentyourlabel'sstickingoutat
thebackofyourjumperalotofpeoplewerecomplainingaboutthe
teacherbutIstuckupforherareyougoingtostickaroundafterthe
classhisteethstickoutabitIwishIhadn'tputmysuitonbecauseI
reallystuckoutlikeasorethumbnobodyreallystickstothespeed
limitI'mstuckonthisquestionshe'sverystuckinherownwayof
doingthings

7 Collocations

Complete the sentences with the missing collocations from page 16 of the Coursebook.

1. He comes from quite a .... background. His parents were quite wealthy and he went to a top private school.

2. I didn't have a particularly .... background. I came to Christianity through a friend I met at college.

3. I've got very .... tastes when it comes to music. I like anything from heavy metal to Mozart.

4. It is a bit of an .... taste. A lot of people don't really like it when they first eat it.

5. The financial scandal badly .... the Prime Minister's reputation for probity.

6. The area is .... an unwarranted reputation for crime and violence.

7. They're so inflexible about how they interpret the regulations. They won't .... the rules for anyone.

8. People aren't supposed to use their mobiles when driving, but they just openly .... the law and the police do absolutely nothing about it.

9. Winning the award really .... my career. Instead of me chasing work, people were contacting me.

10. Although I'm doing a degree in history, I'd really like to .... a career in journalism when I finish university.

8 Emphatic structures

Rewrite the sentences using the words in bold so that they are more emphatic.

1. They mess about all the time. **forever**
   They .... about.

2. He talked to me for ages about his new girlfriend.
   going
   He .... about his new
   girlfriend.

3. He doesn't sit still. He just fidgets.
   won't / constantly
   He .... for a second.
   He ....

4. He only studies and nothing else. **all**
   .... study.

5. They didn't do anything – apart from whinge. **only**
   The .... whinge.

6. She just paints her nails and tries to look beautiful.
   complete / paint
   She .... bimbo. All
   .... her nails and try to look
   beautiful.

9 Continuous tenses

Complete the sentences with the correct continuous form of the verb in brackets.

1. A: I .... if anyone fancied going out later?
   (wonder)
   B: Yeah, I'd be up for doing something.

2. The last teacher I had was so boring! He
   .... constantly .... about
   grammar! (drone on)

3. A: Why did you yell at him? He's only little.
   B: Listen, I know he didn't mean to break the thing,
   but he .... with it after I'd told him to
   stop. It was just the last straw. He ....
   me .... all day and I've had enough.
   (fiddle, wind up)

4. Ignore him! He .... just ....
   stupid. (be)

5. His English is amazing. He must .... for
   years! (study)

10 Key words for writing: *following, subsequently, after* and *afterwards*

All of these words have a similar meaning. Look at these examples and notice the different ways they are used.

Following the introduction of the new laws against sexual discrimination, there was an increase in the number of women who were appointed to management positions. (*After* is also possible in this case. *Following* is more formal.)

I moved to Holland in 2002 and I met my wife the *following* year.

The company lost 5 per cent of its market share. *Subsequently*, they fired their sales executive, but the company still went bankrupt.

After graduating from university, I worked for a merchant bank.

After I worked for them, I did a master's in finance.

I usually go swimming straight *after* work.

I've got to work this evening, but we could meet up *afterwards*. My shift finishes at nine.

Complete the sentences with the words above.

1. I started work immediately .... leaving
   school – and .... came to bitterly regret
   it!

2. The singer was rushed to hospital on Thursday
   evening, but died shortly ....

3. My name was directly .... yours on
   the list.

4. In this chapter, I shall be looking at work patterns in
   Britain, and in the .... chapters I consider
   how they contrast with those in Europe.

5. .... the failed assassination attempt, several
   men were arrested, though most were ....
   released without charge.

6. He got sacked .... a number of complaints
   of sexual harassment. He .... sued the
   company for unfair dismissal, but his claim was
   rejected. We didn't hear from him again
   .... !

7. .... the fire, there was a police
   investigation. .... the findings of the report
   were published, the company instigated a number
   of changes. .... , smoking was banned in
   the building.

2 Work and office politics

1 Fears and worries

Complete the sentences with the pairs of words in the box.

broach + catch	own up + lose
confront + deny	say + take
discuss + end up	tell + leave

1. I can't .... my wife about it. I'm petrified she'd .... me.

2. He's very moody. I'm worried that if I .... the subject of a pay rise, I'll .... him on the wrong day!

3. There's no way I can .... it with my manager. I'm worried I'd .... getting the sack!

4. I really wanted to .... something to her about how I felt, but I was scared she'd .... it the wrong way.

5. I know I ought to .... him about it, but I'm scared he'd just .... it – and that'd make me look stupid!

6. I should just .... to it and get it over with, but I'm petrified he'd .... all respect for me if I did.

2 Adverb–adjective collocations

Complete the sentences with adverbs. The first two letters are given.

1. Ph........................... , it's very demanding. You have to be very fit.

2. It's an in........................... tedious job, but the money's great.

3. As a subject, it's de........................... dull. I couldn't stand it.

4. It's im........................... rewarding on a personal level.

5. Fi........................... , it's very rewarding. I could retire at 45.

6. It's a hi........................... stressful job. You burn out quickly.

7. He's very po...........................-conscious. He's a Tory party member.

8. He's ac........................... gifted. He got a degree at 19.

3 Make and do

Complete the sentences with make or do and the nouns in the box.

accounts	decision	study
business	note	tax return
changes	photocopying	
contacts	sacrifices	

1. I didn't have time to think about it. I just had to .... a snap ....

2. We used to .... a lot of .... in the UK, but we've been slowly squeezed out of the market there over the last few years.

3. Can I borrow your pen? I just need to .... a .... of the date and time we agreed.

4. I'm not happy working such long hours, but you have to .... if you want to get ahead in your career.

5. Remind me I need to .... my .... this week and get it off so they can work out how much I'm supposed to pay!

6. You need to get out there and network more, ... a few more .... with people you might be able to do business with.

7. I'm not sufficiently convinced by these figures. I think we're going to have to .... a more in-depth .... of the market.

8. I'm hopeless at maths, so I get my wife to .... all the company .... She's good at making sure the books balance.

9. The company is going to have to .... some pretty drastic .... if we're not going to end up making a loss this year.

10. I get sick of always being asked to .... all the .... for everyone. I spend half my life on that machine!

4 I don't know

Complete each sentence with ONE word.

1. A: So why did the contract fall through?

   B: It's a long story! I don't know .... to begin.

2. I don't know .... you expect me to do about it! You got yourself into this mess – you get yourself out of it!

3. I sweated blood to get that report finished and he didn't even say thank you! I don't know .... I bother!

4. It was quite a strange letter they sent. I don't know .... best to respond to it, really.

5. I don't know .... they think they're playing at, suddenly changing their offer like that. I'll be talking to our lawyers about it!

6. I just don't know .... I should try and stick my new job out and hope it gets easier or resign now!

5 Describing people you work with

Complete the sentences with these words.

adapt	disturbing	gets on	hurtful	raving
chase	favourites	goes	mince	

1. He's very stuck in his ways and he finds it difficult to .... to change.

2. She doesn't .... her words. She gets right to the point.

3. He often doesn't even realise he's said anything ....

4. She doesn't take sides or have any ....

5. One moment he's fine and the next he starts ranting and .... over something silly.

6. She doesn't make you feel you're .... her if you want to talk. She's not at all standoffish.

7. She just .... with things. You don't have to .... her up all the time.

8. What he says .... , and he's always breathing down your neck to make sure you do it the way he wants.

Match the adjectives in the box with the people described above.

approachable	direct	even-handed	insensitive
conscientious	domineering	inflexible	moody

Language note

Dominate is a verb. We say *He's dominated by his mother*, but not *His mother's ~~dominating~~*. The adjective is *domineering*. We also say things like *He always dominates the conversation* and *She lets her work dominate her life.*

6 Keyword: *target*

Complete the sentences with the collocations of target in the box.

achieving	deliberately	meet	short
ambitious	exceed	modest	
carefully	long-term	principal	

1. They had to get rid of him. They set him some very .... sales targets in his first year, but he didn't even .... those.

2. It was a great year. We set ourselves some pretty .... targets for growth and we actually managed to .... them.

3. We need a .... targeted marketing campaign so we hit our .... target audience of single thirty-something females.

4. When we started the business our initial goal was to break even after two years, but our .... target is to become the biggest company in the sector and we're well on the way to .... it.

5. We've fallen .... of our financial targets, so we're going to have to make cutbacks next year.

6. They should stop fast food companies .... targeting children with their advertising.

We also use target to mean something we shoot at or aim to hurt. Now complete these sentences with the words in the box.

hit	intended	legitimate	off	soft

7. Terrorists see the army as a .... target, because they say they are at war.

8. The most despicable thing about suicide bombers is that they always .... such .... targets – vulnerable unarmed people.

9. Apparently, the bombers made a mistake. The .... target was a politician.

10. He should've scored, but his shot was miles .... target.

Writing: Punctuation and spelling

1 Reading

Read the text about punctuation rules. Underline any information which is new for you.

2 Correct or incorrect punctuation?

Decide which sentences are correctly punctuated. Correct the badly punctuated sentences.

1. If I were you I'd learn how to use comma's properly.

2. Ken told us we should talk to Russ about it – as if he would know!

3. Your manager told me and I quote, if you don't like it you know where the door is!

4. He's a lovely guy: very easy going.

5. Writing, which is badly punctuated, is often taken as a sign of ignorance.

6. I feel I am suitable for the post for a variety of reasons; I have ten years experience in the field, I possess the relevant qualifications and I am keen to extend my horizons.

7. I will forward the files later if that's OK with you.

8. Admittedly I was partly to blame but I still feel I was slightly hard done by.

9. 'I'll meet you behind the shed,' he whispered.

10. The deal, which had provisionally been agreed in Oslo last summer, now looks to be dead.

3 Common spelling mistakes

Decide which words are spelled correctly. Correct the spelling mistakes.

1. independant
2. seperate
3. enviroment
4. calender
5. systematic
6. developement
7. recieve
8. exagerratted
9. accessible
10. doable
11. grammer
12. tendancy
13. wierd
14. fulfillment
15. dissertation
16. atributes
17. priveleged
18. wintry
19. acommodation
20. recurrence

Punctuation 'rules'

Commas

Commas are often used in quite personal ways to signal a mental pause. However, the following are commonly agreed uses:

Lists of words

He's got big, bushy eyebrows.

To separate extra, non-defining information

I had to wait weeks for my order, which was very annoying.
The duty manager, who was new to your firm, was very unhelpful.

If you remove any of the information between the commas, the sentence still makes complete sense. Where information can't be removed, then we don't use commas. For example:

I spoke to the man who was on the front desk, but he was useless.

After certain adverbials at the beginning of a sentence

Strictly speaking, you are in the wrong.
Anyway, I must sign off as I need to get on with some work.
Obviously, we shall reimburse you fully.

Apostrophes

Apostrophes are frequently misused. They should only be used to show that there are letters missing, or that a thing belongs to someone or something else mentioned. There is no apostrophe in *problems* in this example:

This is one of the main problems facing the government.

Colons and semi-colons

Colons are generally used to signal the beginning of an extended list or an exemplification. The list will often be whole sentences or expressions. Semi-colons are used to divide expressions and clauses in a list:

I made several requests: that all the rubbish was removed; that a notice was put up to deter dumping; and that the council repair the damage done to my property. However, nothing has been done.

Dashes and hyphens

Dashes, like commas, are used to add extra comments to the middle or end of a sentence. They are more common in informal writing. Hyphens often – but not always – join two words to make a compound word. There appear to be no rules to govern which compound words have a hyphen and which don't. This means that two people can spell the same word differently, e.g. *cut-throat* and *cutthroat*.

3 Describing places

1 Describing areas

Decide if either one or both of the words in italics are possible.

1. The area has become a complete *no-go / rough* area thanks to all the gang warfare between the drug dealers.

2. This place is absolutely *sleepy / dead*.

3. We had dinner in the restaurant at the top of this building and could see the whole *skyline / scenery* of the city.

4. The centre is quite *deprived / run-down*. All the old buildings have just ended up as *slums / shanty towns*.

5. We stayed in this really *remote / isolated* village in the mountains. It was miles from *anywhere / nowhere*. You go through some spectacular *scenery / landscape* to get there.

6. It's just this enormous *sprawling / widespread* city, which is beginning to engulf the surrounding villages.

7. Just on the *outskirts / edge* of the city, there's a big *shanty town / slum* built by all the people migrating from the country, setting up all these makeshift shacks.

8. There's *sprawling / widespread* poverty in the countryside, but people are still incredibly welcoming.

2 Better than expected

Complete the sentences with ONE word in each space.

1. I was shocked at the .... of people we saw using drugs.

2. I was amazed at the .... of traffic and pollution there. I didn't think it .... be as bad as it ....

3. It was far .... touristy than I was ....

4. It exceeded my .... really. I thought it'd be a fairly sleepy little town, but it .... out to be quite lively.

5. The tour didn't .... up to our expectations. We thought we'd see far more things than we .... did.

6. They said it was a real let-down. I think they thought it'd .... more exciting than it actually ....

7. I was surprised .... just how difficult it was .... find anyone who spoke English.

8. Don't believe the .... I was really up for going there, but I didn't enjoy it as .... as I expected.

3 Practice

Write similar sentences to those in Exercise 2 using these ideas.

1. I / amazed / cheap / everything

2. I / shocked / amount / poverty / everywhere

3. I / surprised / easy / get around

4. we / shocked / number / crashed cars / by the side of the road

5. I think they / expecting / better / actually

6. it turned out / far / crowded / we thought

7. we thought / enjoy / than / actually

8. I / expecting / disaster / turned out / brilliant

4 Collocations

Match the verbs with the groups of words and expressions they collocate with.

attract	cause	gain	reverse
bow to	enter into	reject	take

1. .... experience / useful insights

2. .... a company's decline / a judgment

3. .... offence / it the wrong way

4. .... tourists / inward investment

5. .... peace talks / a trade agreement

6. .... a great deal of controversy / upset

7. .... public pressure / diplomatic pressure

8. .... criticism / a proposal / an offer

5 Comparing places

Complete the sentences with these words.

compared	league	nowhere	times
comparison	miles	tenfold	

1. The food here is .... near as good as it is back home. Everything's so stodgy here.

2. The beaches there are .... better. Golden sands and crystal clear water – and they're almost deserted!

3. The cost of living there is unbelievable. Everything is about three .... more expensive than it is in Poland.

4. I can't believe people believe that Cardiff is on a par with Edinburgh. Really, they're not even in the same .... !

5. When it comes to nightlife, there's no .... Istanbul just has so much more to offer than Ankara.

6. There's been a .... increase in the number of tourists visiting over the last few years.

7. The hotel we stayed in in York was fairly basic, but it was a palace .... to the one we stayed in in London. That place was a complete dump!

6 Movements

Complete the sentences with these words.

criticised	enjoyed	infighting	peak
emerged	handful	momentum	petered out

1. By the 80s, the movement no longer .... the support of most of those it claimed to be representing.

2. When the movement first .... , it only consisted of a .... of members, but it has grown massively since then.

3. The movement was at its .... in the late 1960s, but had more or less .... by the 90s.

4. The separatist movement has been dogged by ....

5. The home-schooling movement has been gaining considerable .... over the last few years.

6. The movement has basically been .... because of its covert support for terrorism.

7 Word building

Complete the sentences with the correct forms of the words given.

1. **demonstrate**
   A small group of .... staged a rowdy protest outside the courtroom before the police moved in and broke the .... up.

2. **deprive**
   The area is one of the most .... in the country. Indeed, the .... is so severe that for many the basic needs of life are barely being met.

3. **attend**
   Following several years in which .... dropped to alarmingly low levels, I'm pleased to say that the two most recent conferences have both been very well .... Hopefully, we have done enough to persuade all those in .... at the Madrid event to book early for next year.

4. **publicise**
   The couple's wedding is rumoured to have taken place last week, though their .... have refused to confirm or deny anything. This reticence to engage with the media has failed to prevent a blaze of .... and fevered speculation.

5. **decide**
   Having long been infamous for their chronic .... , the UN have finally managed to act .... for once! Let's hope it is not a .... they will come to regret!

6. **benefit**
   This latest breakthrough could prove to be very .... to all manner of patients, though perhaps the main .... will be those suffering from cancer.

8 Pronunciation: word class and word stress

Underline the syllable which carries the main stress in these words.

1. <u>pho</u>tograph
2. photographer
3. photogenic
4. economy
5. economist
6. economical
7. technician
8. technicality
9. technical
10. permit (v)
11. permit (n)
12. impermissible

Now use a dictionary to check your ideas.

9 Social and economic problems

Complete the sentences with the correct form of these verbs.

attract	detract	put forward
be dogged	erupt	repair
be rejected	foster	start
be seen	provoke	

1. The organisation .... by controversy ever since it first emerged in the 1970s.

2. The government .... a proposal for constitutional reform last year, but it .... roundly ....

3. I don't think we should accept the gifts they're offering. They could .... as a potential source of corruption.

4. The fact that some designers have decided to allow fur back onto the catwalk this season .... a lot of media attention.

5. A huge row .... between two rival factions within the party over who the next leader should be.

6. The erection of the monument .... major controversy, with many dubbing it an eyesore and calling for its removal.

7. The charity's work there helps .... good relations between the two countries.

8. Admittedly, there were some demonstrators who were intent on causing trouble, but that shouldn't .... from the real issue here – the violence of the police towards peaceful protestors.

9. It's going to take a long time to .... the damage done by the No vote in the last referendum.

10. Aid workers in the region .... a campaign to vaccinate ten million children against polio.

Now complete these expressions with ONE word from the sentences above.

a. The plan was .... rejected.

b. It's one potential .... of revenue.

c. The news attracted a lot of media ....

d. The group split into two rival ....

e. Some protestors were clearly intent .... causing trouble.

f. That shouldn't detract from the main .... here.

10 Key words for writing: *before* and *after*

There are many different ways to refer to the time before or after an event. Look at these examples:

Prior to becoming an MP, Mark Sanders worked for local government.

The claim was first made on television in June 2003, and was *then* repeated in several *subsequent* news briefings.

Complete the sentences with these words.

due	preceding	subsequent
following	previous	subsequently
moment	prior	

1. It was revealed that several contra-indications had been reported in trials .... to the drug's launch, but the concerns had been brushed aside.

2. The couple married in August 2002 and from that .... on, they argued continually.

3. The weeks .... the election were very busy as everyone was out canvassing votes.

4. You will be paid in .... course, after your invoice has been processed by accounts.

5. .... months of uncertainty about the future of the department, I am delighted to announce the launch of this new initiative.

6. The Harry Potter books proved extremely successful and were .... made into films.

7. People reported having seen the suspects in the area on two .... occasions.

8. He was first found guilty of fraud in 1985 and was charged with the same crime on seven .... occasions.

Join these sentences using the words in brackets. Make any other necessary changes.

9. They decided to sell the farm. Before this, they had been having problems. (prior to)

10. He appeared in a reality TV show. After this, he received many offers of work. (following on from)

11. There was an initial exploratory dig. Excavations carried out after this revealed the foundations of an ancient city. (subsequent to)

12. I moved to Leeds in 2004. For three years before my move, I held various posts in the Economics department at the University of Dundee. (preceding)

4 The law

1 Keywords: *law / laws*

Complete the sentences with these words.

above	introduce	required	unenforceable
banning	lawless	stands	uphold
breakdown	offence	taking	
flouting	relaxing	tightening	

1. It's crazy, because as the law currently .... , you can get married and have kids before you can vote!

2. You're .... by law to register with the local police within three days of arrival in the country.

3. In the wake of the hurricane, there was a complete .... in law and order.

4. It's scary. It's a pretty .... kind of place, so if you're rich out there, you're basically .... the law. You can literally do whatever you want, so some people act with complete impunity.

5. The government is planning to .... a new law making it a criminal .... to incite racial hatred.

6. It was generally felt that the police weren't doing enough to .... the law and in the end, people started .... the law into their own hands and forming vigilante groups to patrol the streets.

7. The thing is, it's an .... law. The police can't arrest every single person who uses their mobile while driving, can they?

8. They're talking about .... the drinking laws, and letting pubs and bars stay open later.

9. They're talking about .... the law to prevent similar incidents happening again in the future.

10. They passed a law last year .... smoking in all public places, but you still see plenty of people openly .... the law and lighting up in bars or restaurants!

Language note

There is no fixed rule for whether collective nouns should be treated as singular or plural. They can basically be seen as both. However, some collective nouns tend to be more commonly used as singular nouns, some as plural. Look at these examples:

The government has promised to review the gun laws next year.
The jury still *hasn't* reached a verdict.
The audience was quite hostile.
The police have warned the public to be on their guard.
Manchester United are having a difficult season.
The couple have decided to adopt.

2 Expressions starting with *to*

Match the expression beginnings with the endings.

1. to add   a. the record straight
2. to cut   b. a long story short
3. to top   c. you the truth
4. to say   d. it all off
5. to tell   e. insult to injury
6. to set   f. the least

Now complete the sentences with the expressions above.

7. There seems to have been a misunderstanding here, so just .... , I'm actually Ms Jenkins to you – not Mrs, OK?

8. In the space of a week, I broke my leg, lost my job, got dumped and then – .... – my dog died!

9. .... , I didn't really like the city. I found it scary!

10. You know how useless I am with computers, so I was slightly confused, ... !

11. The whole situation got quite complicated but .... , let's just say it didn't exactly end happily for me!

12. The builder broke the boiler while he was installing the kitchen and then .... , he actually tried to charge me for fixing it! I was less than happy, to say the least!

3 Collocations

Match the verbs with the groups of words and expressions they collocate with.

charge	exploit	file
commit	fight	resort

1. .... to underhand means / to the courts
2. .... a heinous crime / an offence
3. .... high legal fees / extortionate amounts
4. .... a legal battle / a custody battle
5. .... legal loopholes / naive clients
6. .... for divorce / for bankruptcy

Now match these verbs with the groups of words and expressions they collocate with.

be awarded	guard	introduce
conduct	infringe	take

7. .... them to court / out an injunction
8. .... against terrorism / against corruption
9. .... an investigation / court proceedings
10. .... £5,000 in damages / custody
11. .... civil liberties / basic human rights
12. .... new laws / stringent safety rules

Which adjectives above went with the words *crime, fees, battle, laws* and *rules*? Which prepositions went with *file, resort* and *guard*?

4 Formal written language

Replace the less formal words in the sentences with the correct form of these more formal words.

be advised	overleaf	regret
be directed	previous	result
complete	purchase	
matter	refer to	

1. I have now *finished* all the contracts regarding the *buying* of the property.
2. I'm *sorry* to inform you that you are liable for all the damages that *came* from the accident.
3. I wrote to you *before* concerning this *thing*, but you have still not responded to my queries.
4. Please *look at* my notes regarding this *on the other side of this page*.
5. You *really should* take out insurance in case of emergencies or cancellations. Any complaints should *be told* to the manager in writing.

5 Modals

Complete the conversations with modal verbs and the verbs in brackets in the correct form. You may need to use a negative.

Conversation 1

A: I (1) .... her at least six times to bring some kind of proof of ID, but of course she didn't. So then we (2) .... on the plane. (remind, get)

B: You (3) .... furious with her. (be)

A: Believe me, I was so mad I (4) .... her. (throttle)

B: I think I (5) .... her behind – just to teach her a lesson. (leave)

A: Yeah, maybe I (6) .... I definitely (7) .... next time!

Conversation 2

A: To be honest, we thought everything (8) .... open as normal, but nearly all the restaurants were closed. We just (9) .... it! We (10) .... about five miles looking for somewhere which was serving food. (be, believe, walk)

B: But you managed to find something?

A: Yeah, eventually – this tiny little place. But they said the only thing they (11) .... us was an omelette as they were about to close. In any other circumstances, I (12) .... looking, but we were so desperate we said yes. (serve, carry on)

B: I (13) .... I (14) .... the same. So was it all right? (imagine, do)

A: Yeah, it (15) .... worse. They were actually very nice people and they gave us a drink on the house, so it was OK. (be)

6 Word building: adjectives to nouns

Complete the collocations with the correct noun form of the adjectives.

1. accept .... (liable)
2. have a lot of .... (responsible)
3. be a total .... (hypocritical)
4. not show much .... (grateful)
5. feel out of your .... (deep)
6. be involved in endless .... (litigious)
7. suffer from a .... (able)
8. the negative consequences of .... (moral)

Writing: Letters of application

1 Sample letter

Complete the letter with the words in the box.

committed	possess	teamwork
currently	recruitment	wish
extend	reputation	
interpersonal	role	

Dear Sir / Madam,

I was sent your recent advertisement for a deputy manager at your Croydon venue by a (1) ... agency and am writing to apply for the position.

I am (2) ... employed as assistant manager at 'Atlanta' in Southampton, where I have been working for three years. Prior to this, I worked in a wine bar and gained a degree of managerial experience in my (3) ... as duty manager.

As you will see from my enclosed CV, I have experience in all areas of retail management – from stock control to staffing levels. I (4) ... all relevant certificates, including the national licensee certificate and the door supervisor licence.

I feel that my greatest strengths lie in my (5) ... skills and the ability to encourage (6) ... among my staff. I am always (7) ... to whatever challenges I accept and have the confidence to face both success and disappointment, and learn from the experiences.

I am looking to (8) ... my experience by working in a larger venue with an emphasis on catering and dance. I am also attracted by the (9) ... of your company for staff and managerial progression.

Should you need further details or (10) ... to arrange an interview, please do not hesitate to contact me.

I look forward to hearing from you.

Yours faithfully,

Beresford Hammond

2 Collocations

Choose the correct word.

1. I am applying for the post of *vice / deputy* manager in your Plymouth branch.
2. *Prior / Before* to working for British Gas, I worked for British Telecom.
3. I am able to drive in the United Kingdom as I possess a full European driving *test / licence*.
4. Your company has an excellent record in managerial *career / progression*.
5. I also *carry / hold* a Master's degree in Botany.
6. I would look forward to facing new *challenges / hopes*, were I to be offered the post.
7. I trust you will feel this experience is *relevant / necessary* to the post.
8. I have *added / enclosed* a reference from my last employer.

3 Useful expressions

Complete each sentence with ONE word.

1. I am writing in .... to your recent advertisement for a French translator.
2. I feel I would be .... for the post for a .... of reasons.
3. .... you require any further references, I would be happy to .... them.
4. Should you require any further information or .... to arrange an interview, please do not .... to contact me.
5. Should any vacancies become .... , please contact me at the .... opportunity.
6. I am available for interview at any ....
7. I look forward to .... from you.

4 Writing a covering letter

Write a covering letter with your CV. Think about:

- where you saw the post advertised
- what relevant work experience you have
- what relevant qualifications you have
- what you can bring to the job – and what you hope to get out of it
- what interests you about this particular company

Grammar: Time adverbials

1 Perfect tenses and time adverbials

Complete the sentences with the words in the box in the correct perfect tense form. Underline the adverbials.

build up	get	put	speak
deteriorate	hand in	receive	
do	make up	say	

1. By the time I finished university, I .... debts of £20,000.

2. Where are they? They should .... here by now.

3. I doubt we .... the work by Friday. It's looking more likely to be Tuesday.

4. If he .... his mind by next week, I'm just going to take the matter into my own hands.

5. Once we .... your application, we will acknowledge receipt.

6. As soon as I .... to him, I'll let you know what the story is.

7. I'd been thinking about quitting my job for ages, and as soon as I .... my notice, it was a real weight off my shoulders.

8. As soon as I .... it, I realised .... my foot in it.

9. Over the past few years, things .... a lot.

2 Continuous tenses and adverbials

Complete the sentences with the words in brackets in the correct continuous tense form. One sentence will need to be negative.

1. We met in Hong Kong. I .... there at the time. (work)

2. This time tomorrow I .... myself on the beach. (sun)

3. Things .... for a while last year as far as sales were concerned, but I think we .... a losing battle at the moment. (look up, fight)

4. Over recent years, more and more people .... to the reality of debt and bankruptcy. (face up)

5. I do worry about what they .... children nowadays. (teach)

6. He must've nicked it while I .... ! (look)

Language note

When we talk about general trends in society that are happening now, we tend to use *nowadays* or *these days* rather than *at the moment*. We use *at the moment* (but not *nowadays*) to describe temporary situations. For example, we don't say ~~I'm looking for a job nowadays~~. Instead, we say *I'm looking for a job at the moment.*

3 Other time adverbials

Decide if either one or both of the adverbial expressions in italics are appropriate and correct.

1. Men don't seem to hold doors open *these days / at the moment*. It was all very different *in my day / when I was a girl*. It's such a pity!

2. I was just browsing really, but they had a fantastic offer on a holiday in the Maldives, so I booked it *there and then / at that moment*.

3. A: I'm dreading the speaking exam on Friday.
   B: Don't worry. I'm sure you'll be all right *that day / on the day*.

4. *To begin with / At first*, everyone was a bit wary of each other, but *before long / shortly* we'd broken the ice and were all chatting away.

5. Please take a seat, Mr Williams. I'll be with you *in one moment / shortly*.

6. We were walking round in circles for hours, but *at last / in the end* we managed to find the place.

7. A: *At last / Finally!*
   B Sorry. Have you been waiting *long / a long time*?
   A: I was beginning to worry you'd been knocked over by a bus or something! Never mind. If we get a move on, we can still get to the cinema *in time / on time* to see the start of the film.

8. I'm not going to be in on Tuesday, so I'll see you *the next day / the day after*.

9. I am *nowadays / currently* working for a merchant bank here in Frankfurt, but I am looking for opportunities to work in the City of London *in the near future / someday soon*.

10. *Up until recently / Up until now*, I'd never even thought of getting married.

5 Food

1 Ingredients

Put the words in the box into four groups of four.

cinnamon	dill	oregano	sage
cloves	fennel	parsnip	thyme
cumin	fig	pomegranate	turmeric
date	nectarine	radish	turnip

Fruits	Herbs	Spices	Vegetables
....	....	....	....
....	....	....	....
....	....	....	....
....	....	....	....

 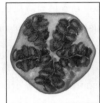 

| **fennel** | **pomegranate** | **turnips** |

2 Recipe

Complete the recipe with these words.

coat	serve	sprinkle	warm
evaporates	simmer	squeeze	
pour	slice	stir	

Chicken Marsala

Take two large chicken (or turkey) breasts and
(1) ... them into thin pieces. Then, over medium heat,
(2) ... a few tablespoons of olive oil in a large pan for
a few seconds, taking care not to burn it. (3) ... the
chicken pieces with a little salt and pepper. Then
(4) ... the chicken pieces completely with flour and
place them in the pan, turning them from time to
time. Next, (5) ... the juice from one lemon and add.
Once the chicken is basically done, (6) ... a glass of
Sicilian Marsala wine over it. (7) ... the mixture
gently. Let it (8) ... for a couple of minutes to ensure
the sauce thickens and the alcohol (9) ... . Add some
coarsely-chopped parsley and a few capers and it's
ready to (10) ... .

3 Food and dietary problems

Match the sentences with the follow-up comments.

1. I developed some kind of allergy to cats. ☐
2. I used to be, literally, clinically obese! ☐
3. The curry gave me awful wind. ☐
4. I had dreadful diarrhoea. ☐
5. After my son was born, I was terribly constipated. ☐
6. I threw up about six times during the night. ☐
7. My stomach was rumbling really badly. ☐
8. I just absolutely stuffed myself. ☐

a. Honestly, I was just constantly in and out of the loo!
b. I think some of the prawns must've been off.
c. Honestly, I weighed 25 stone at one point!
d. Honestly, I couldn't go for almost a fortnight!
e. I had to loosen my belt before I could stand up!
f. Honestly, I just couldn't stop farting! It was so embarrassing!
g. Honestly, I just couldn't stop sneezing! It was awful!
h. I hadn't eaten since the early morning, you see.

4 Talking about diets

Complete the sentences with these words.

crash	piled	stick to	wind
fad	religiously	stink	
lethargic	shed	wheat-free	

1. I've been on this diet for a month now, but it's just making me feel so .... all the time. I've lost all my get up and go.

2. I must've tried every dieting .... , but I haven't been able to .... any of them!

3. I followed that diet .... for a while, but then my breath started to .... and I got terrible .... , so I gave up!

4. She suffers from allergies, so she's on a .... diet.

5. He went on this .... diet and .... about 20 kilos in a month – but then when he stopped, he .... the pounds back on!

5 Quantifiers

If you add a *splash* of *wine* to a sauce, you add a small amount.

Complete the sentences with these quantifiers.

bite	drop	pinch	slice
drag	hint	sip	spoonful

1. I think it could do with a .... of salt.

2. Would you like a .... more wine?

3. It's not too spicy. It's just got a .... of chilli.

4. Would you like another .... of ice cream?

5. Can I tempt you with one more .... of cake?

6. Shall we get a .... to eat?

7. Can I just have a .... of your cigarette? I'm actually trying to give up, but I'm struggling a bit.

8. What does your juice taste like? Can I have a .... and see?

We often use these words in replies to questions.

A: Would you like some ice cream?

B: Yeah OK, just a spoonful.

6 Expressions with *of*

Choose the more natural word to make expressions with *of*.

1. Don't worry! I'd take whatever he says with a *spoonful / pinch* of salt. Honestly, he's just scaremongering.

2. I left the pan on by mistake. Luckily, I got back in the *nick / stroke* of time before the whole kitchen caught fire!

3. There are a whole *host / line* of reasons why I'm vegetarian.

4. Broccoli is supposed to give you *bags / piles* of energy.

5. She was in *streams / floods* of tears after the burglary.

6. There have been several *miscarriages / mistakes* of justice.

7. He committed a *string / line* of offences.

8. There is a *piece / grain* of truth to the accusation.

9. There's been *a spate / an amount* of burglaries in the area recently.

10. It's the latest in a long *line / string* of scandals to beset the legal profession.

7 Food issues

Complete the texts with ONE word in each space.

Genetically modified foods

Many people worry about GM foods because they (1) ... it as meddling with the very stuff of life. They are concerned that these foods have not (2) ... rigorously tested and are potentially dangerous for (3) ... the environment and our own health. They fear GM crops will pollinate wild plants, creating super-weeds resistant (4) ... herbicides, and also increase resistance to antibiotics in humans. Many feel governments are pandering to the demands of big business (5) ... approving the production of GM products in the (6) ... of widespread opposition. However, supporters of GM contend that there is much scaremongering and (7) ... actual proof of any health hazards. They argue the foods have been thoroughly scrutinised and have gained (8) ... for consumption from a wide variety of government and scientific bodies. They suggest that (9) ... from damaging the environment, GM crops will reduce the (10) ... for pesticides, have a positive impact (11) ... biodiversity, and at the same time increase yields.

Intensive farming

There have been increasing concerns (12) ... the growth of intensive farming techniques using huge greenhouses. Campaigners argue (13) ... they are blights on the landscape as huge swathes of land are (14) ... in plastic. They fear that overproduction is exhausting the land and could (15) ... turn the areas where it takes place (16) ... desert. However, the farmers counter that the benefits far (17) ... the drawbacks, as the greenhouses allow cultivation in areas which would (18) ... be barren. They create jobs in deprived areas and (19) ... consumers with fruit and vegetables out of (20) ... .

Look back through the text and find:

• adverbs that go with *tested, dangerous* and *scrutinised*
• adjectives that go with *business, opposition* and *impact*
• verbs that go with *plants, demands, land, benefits* and *jobs*

8 Food idioms

Complete the idioms with the words in the box.

bread	butter	cakes	icing
breadline	cake	eggs	salt

The area of food and cooking has given the English language a lot of different idioms and metaphors. Many of these involve food that is common in the UK. For instance, you can say that something you find very easy is (1) *a piece of ...* , while something that happens to make an already good situation even better is (2) *the ... on the cake*. If a product sells very well and very quickly, you can tell people it's (3) *selling like hot ...* . If you describe something as your (4) *...and butter*, it means it's your main source of income, whilst people who are really poor and who only have a very basic level of income are (5) *living on the ...* . If you want somebody to do something for you, you might need to (6) *... them up* beforehand – be especially nice to them, so as to persuade them to do what you want! When you don't always believe everything somebody says and are sceptical about how truthful they are being, you (7) *take the* information *with a pinch of ...* . Finally, when you want to warn someone not to invest all their hopes in one person or one course of action, you can tell them not to (8) *put all their ... in one basket*.

Now cover the idioms above and complete each of these sentences by adding the whole idiom.

a. He's potentially a very important client, so we'd better take him out and wine and dine him and just generally try to ....

b. I'm self-employed. I do some consultancy work, but my .... comes from providing training to firms.

c. I don't know why I was so worried about giving blood. There was nothing to it. Honestly, it was ....

d. I'm trying to save as much as I can. I don't want to spend my retirement .... !

e. It was an interesting article, but it was just taken from the web, so you do need to ....

9 Key words for writing: *so as (not) to / in order (not) to / with the sole purpose of*

These linking expressions can replace the infinitive with *to* and emphasise the purpose of an action.

Book early *so as to* avoid disappointment.

We took the earlier train *so as not to* be late.

In order to assess your claim, we need you to complete the attached form.

He joined the company *with the sole purpose of* planning the robbery.

The audience were asked not to applaud after every act *so as not to / in order not to* disturb the performers.

Complete the sentences with these words.

as	in	not	not	order	with

1. Please attend a meeting at 10.30 .... order to discuss salary increases for the coming year.

2. The letter was leaked .... the sole purpose of embarrassing the government.

3. We herein offer an immediate refund so as .... to inconvenience you further.

4. Food acceptable to both religions was provided so .... not to offend either family.

5. The council is making cutbacks in .... to save taxpayers' money.

6. We shall send the replacement immediately in order .... to cause you any further inconvenience.

Join these sentences using the words in brackets. Make any other necessary changes.

7. They tabled the amendment. The only thing they wanted was to bring down the government. (the sole purpose)

8. Please arrive promptly at 2.30. We do not want to waste time. (so as)

9. Language students should ideally read a great deal. This will extend their vocabulary. (in order)

10. Please come to the police station tomorrow afternoon. You have to complete your statement. (in order)

11. We should eat less fat. This will reduce cholesterol and the dangers of a heart attack. (so as)

6 Disasters

1 Disasters in the news

Complete the texts with the words in the boxes.

Text 1

airlift	drop	lows	rationed
blanket	famine	plagues	
crops	harvest	rainfall	

Drought worsens

The worsening drought has led to a state of emergency being declared across the country. The effect of months of low (1) ... and freak hot weather has led to a dramatic (2) ... in water levels. Several major rivers have either seen record (3) ... or have dried up.

Fears of a (4) ... are growing as farmers have been unable to (5) ... anything this autumn. Not only have the vast majority of (6) ... failed, but farms have also been blighted by (7) ... of locusts. Environmental groups have blamed deforestation and global warming.

As a result of the acute shortage, water is now being (8) ... , with limits placed on water available for agricultural purposes and a (9) ... ban being imposed on hosepipe use. Meanwhile, the army has started to (10) ... water, food and medical supplies into remote areas.

Text 2

bring	evacuated	razed	stretched
charred	raging	sparked	suspicion

Forest fires continue to spread

Forest fires are today still (11) ... across large parts of the north of the country. Firefighters have been working through the night in an attempt to (12) ... the worst fires under control, but a spokesperson has claimed that the fire service is being (13) ... to breaking point. Hundreds of people have been (14) ... from the villages most at risk, and many are feared dead. This morning, the (15) ... body of an elderly man was retrieved from a burnt-out building.

Countless other homes have been (16) ... to the ground, and the fires continue to ravage large areas. The initial blaze is believed to have been (17) ... by a barbecue. However, three men were last night arrested on (18) ... of starting additional fires.

2 Passives (1)

Rewrite the sentences using the words in brackets so that they contain the kind of passive structures common in the news. For example:

They don't think her injuries are life-threatening. (thought)

Her injuries are not thought to be life-threatening.

1. They think the main suspect is English. (thought)
2. They believe the disease is a mutant form of horse influenza. (believed)
3. They think fifty people died in the landslide. (feared)
4. The police think Mitchell has been involved in organised crime for a long time. (suspected)
5. People say Darin was driving at over a hundred miles an hour when the accident occurred. (reported)
6. They don't think the date will be announced for another few weeks. (expected)
7. The police don't think the fires were started deliberately. (thought)
8. They don't think Dr Kirkland obtained consent from his patients to use them in a drug trial. (alleged)

3 Passives (2)

Complete the sentences with the verbs in the box.

blown off	expelled	run over
broken into	held up	sucked up
caught	mugged	

1. Our roof got .... in that big storm.
2. I read in the paper that a cow got .... in the tornado and dumped ten miles away!
3. Sorry we're so late. We got .... at the airport.
4. Our dog got .... on the main road the other week and we had to have it put down.
5. My car got .... last night. They took my CD player and a bag I'd stupidly left on the seat!
6. I got .... at knifepoint when I was on holiday.
7. She got .... from school after getting .... smoking marijuana in the toilets!

4 Asking for charity

Complete the texts with ONE word in each space.

Text 1

I represent an NGO in Central Africa, (1) .... main concern is to provide education and training to health workers who deal with sufferers of HIV/AIDS. We are currently running a campaign to raise £120,000 in (2) .... to provide a mobile unit which is (3) .... of reaching some of the more remote villages in the country. If you would like to become a private (4) .... or your company would be interested in (5) .... a corporate donation, please contact us on 09788200.

Text 2

We are a charity which funds a wide (6) .... of projects to help young people (7) .... disadvantaged backgrounds in Britain. We are currently running a campaign to raise awareness of the issue of runaways and the (8) .... of support and safe housing for them.

Thousands of children run (9) .... from home every year. Sometimes they are undergoing personal traumas and require space from their families for a (10) .... while, but many then return; others are escaping more serious problems of violence and sexual abuse. As well as making people more (11) .... of these children's situations, we are lobbying the government to provide proper refuges (12) .... particularly vulnerable children. If you would like to help with our campaign, for example by distributing leaflets or collecting (13) .... for our petition, complete the form below and send to FREEPOST PO BOX 9799.

Cover the texts and complete the collocations.

Verb–noun

a. .... education   b. .... a project

c. .... awareness   d. .... personal trauma

e. .... serious problems

f. .... the government   g. .... leaflets

h. .... the form

Adjective–noun

i. .... concern   j. .... unit

k. .... villages   l. .... donor

m. .... donation   n. .... backgrounds

o. .... abuse

5 Reporting: verbs and nouns

Complete each of the pairs of sentences with the correct form of a verb in the box or its noun form.

accuse	deny	recommend
allege	persuade	refuse
approve	reassure	~~reject~~

1a. The court ....*rejected*........ his appeal out of hand.

1b. As an aspiring actor, you have to learn to handle ....*rejection*........ .

2a. The report in the newspaper .... that the politician had accepted bribes.

2b. Since the .... of malpractice surfaced, the government has refused to respond.

3a. The star has issued a .... that he has had an affair.

3b. I forgot my password, so I was .... access to the site.

4a. He just .... point blank to tell me what'd happened.

4b. His .... to accept responsibility angers me.

5a. I had to use all my powers of .... to get him to stay.

5b. I tried to .... him to come with us, but he was adamant he didn't want to.

6a. The unions are seeking .... that the merger won't mean job cuts.

6b. We complained about the service and he .... us it wouldn't happen again.

7a. We've finally got .... from management to go ahead with our plans to expand.

7b. Her parents don't .... of us living together.

8a. He was falsely .... of sexual harassment.

8b. The investigation found there were absolutely no grounds for the ....

9a. After assessing the various options, the board .... the takeover to the shareholders.

9b. The committee made several .... , but the government ignored them all.

Writing: Discursive essays

1 | Sample essay

Choose the correct words to complete the text.

1.	a. talk	b. conversation	c. debate	d. row
2.	a. issue	b. idea	c. problem	d. thought
3.	a. halt	b. prohibition	c. ban	d. stop
4.	a. obsession	b. addiction	c. desire	d. likeness
5.	a. gradually	b. sufficiently	c. mainly	d. currently
6.	a. ask	b. demand	c. beg	d. query
7.	a. dangerous	b. detrimental	c. poor	d. contagious
8.	a. cost	b. payment	c. loss	d. debit
9.	a. partial	b. partly	c. half	d. reduced
10.	a. decision	b. possibility	c. situation	d. right

The question of whether the British government should impose a total ban on smoking in all public places has ignited (1) ...... all over the country. It seems that everyone has a standpoint on this (2) ....

On the one hand, we have the belief that a smoke-filled room is both dangerous to health and unpleasant for non-smokers. There is a great deal of medical evidence to support this opinion, and doctors and other medical experts would like to see a total (3) .... There is also the feeling that the taxpayer is paying for the health treatment of smokers who contract diseases because of their (4) ....

On the other hand, there are those who believe that smokers are (5) ...... being squeezed out of the majority of workplaces, restaurants, and so on. There are even those who (6) ...... the medical evidence that supports the dangers of passive smoking. Others cite tradition (is a pub without smoke still a pub?) and the freedom of the individual to do harm to himself should he wish to. They suggest that no government would ever ban alcohol, whatever (7) ...... effects it may have on our health and whatever its (8) ...... to the health service.

Somewhere between these two viewpoints lie those of us who favour a (9) ...... as opposed to a total ban, with a degree of protection for those whose work takes them into smoky areas. In my opinion, the most important question this issue raises is how far the government can (or indeed should) go to protect us. I believe that individuals have the (10) ...... to choose what they do, be it smoking or drinking – as long as those of us who choose not to indulge have the opportunity to go to smoke-free zones.

2 | Vocabulary

Complete the sentences with these words from the text.

cite	ignited	matters	standpoints
evidence	impose	object	
grounds	lies	raises	

1. The issue of whether pubs should be allowed to open for 24 hours can be viewed from several different ....

2. In my opinion, the time has come to .... a total ban on vivisection.

3. Many people .... to the erection of mobile phone masts on schools on the .... that they constitute a health risk.

4. The decision to restrict trial by jury has .... furious debate.

5. However, a ban might make .... worse.

6. The .... clearly points to the need for legislation to restrict the import of livestock.

7. Supporters of a crackdown frequently .... New York as a model of what can be achieved.

8. The most important question this issue .... is how far a ban would impact on personal freedom.

9. The truth probably .... somewhere between these two extreme standpoints.

3 | Writing a short discursive essay

Think of some proposed legislation in your country that you either agree or disagree with. Spend some time thinking about the following:

• how you will show why the topic is important at the moment

• which opinions on the matter you disagree with

• why you disagree with them and what you feel

Next, plan how you are going to paragraph the essay. Finally, write it!

7 | Hair and beauty

1 I wish

Match the sentences with the follow-up comments.

1. I wish I'd had the guts to tell her what I thought of her. ☐
2. I just wish she'd had more of a sense of humour. ☐
3. I wish he wouldn't pick holes in everything I do. ☐
4. I really wish she wouldn't always pick on me. ☐
5. I wish he wasn't so useless around the house. ☐
6. I wish he didn't have such a condescending attitude. ☐

a. I can't stand the way he always talks down to me.
b. It'd be nice if he just washed up once in a while!
c. She was always so serious about everything.
d. He really undermines my confidence.
e. I was so intimidated by her I just bottled it all up.
f. It's always me that gets blamed for every little thing that goes wrong. It's so unfair!

Now complete these sentences with the correct form of the verb in brackets.

7. I wish I .... a bit taller. I hate being so short. (be)
8. I'm really enjoying college, but I wish I .... so busy. It'd be nice to have time for a social life. (be)
9. I wish I .... something to him when I had the chance. I might never meet him again now! (say)
10. God, can't you just stop it! Honestly, I really wish you .... that. It's so annoying! (do)
11. I wish I .... him about it! He's got such a big mouth – and now half the office knows! (tell)
12. I wish I .... such enormous feet. It's nigh-on impossible finding shoes in my size! (have)
13. It worries me how passive my dad is. I sometimes wish he .... actually .... angry about things and .... his temper! (get, lose)

2 Talking about what people look like

Complete the sentences with the words in the box.

bags	delicate	pierced
beer gut	greying	piercing
bloodshot	nicotine-stained	wrinkled

1. He must be in his fifties. He's got .... hair and quite a .... face.
2. He's got this big .... It's a real turn-off!
3. He's got loads of tattoos and a .... nose!
4. He's got these horrible .... fingers.
5. She's got such lovely long .... fingers.
6. She's got amazing .... greeny-blue eyes.
7. I looked like death warmed up! My eyes were all .... and I had great big .... under them!

Now complete these sentences with the words in the box.

boyish	patch	slender	stubble
cheekbones	receding	soulful	stumpy

8. He's one of those irritating guys who's just been blessed with .... good looks!
9. I hate my legs! They're so fat and .... ! I wish I had long .... legs like you!
10. She's gorgeous! She's got these big brown .... eyes.
11. I wish he'd shave more often. He's often got this horrible .... It really prickles!
12. He's got a bald .... on top and his hairline's .... pretty badly!
13. She's a model! She's got beautiful high ....

Language note

greeny-blue eyes: In spoken English, we often add *-y* to a colour like this. It means the eyes are mainly blue, but with some green in them. You can also say *bluey-green*, *greenish-blue* or *blueish-green* – depending on the main colour, of course.

3 Body verbs

Complete the sentences with the pairs of words.

back + went	stomach + rumbling
biting + nails	stretch + legs
eyes + watering	wipe + feet

1. I was starving. My .... was really ....

2. I'm just going to pop out for a little walk, just to .... my .... a bit before dinner.

3. Can you chop the rest of these onions? My .... are .... like mad!

4. I wish I could stop .... my .... Look at them! They're all chewed and horrible!

5. Make sure you .... your .... before you come in. I don't want mud on my floor.

6. I was lifting weights at the gym when my .... just suddenly .... I thought I'd broken it!

4 Idioms: parts of the body

Complete the sentences with the nouns in the box.

arm	ear	guts
blood	eye	mind
brains	face	muscle

1. She's a great designer. She's got a really good .... for colour and form.

2. I've been racking my .... trying to remember the name, but it's completely slipped my ....

3. Chelsea are flexing their financial .... pre-season, spending £130 million on new players.

4. OK, OK. I'll do it. You've twisted my ....

5. Robin tried to put on a brave .... , but I could see that deep down he was really upset.

6. There's quite a lot of bad .... between the two countries – for a whole host of reasons.

7. I should've quit, but I didn't have the ....

8. Your pronunciation is amazing. You must have a very good .... for language.

Language note

If you think someone *has guts*, you think they're brave. You can say people *have balls*, but many think that this is rude. We often say people are *gutless* if they give in easily and don't stand up for what they believe in.

5 Have something done

Complete the sentences using the *have something done* structure in the correct form.

1. I only decided .... because they were actually starting to cause me pain. I wasn't that bothered up until then. (teeth / straighten)

2. I really hate .... at the dentist's, but being a smoker I really need .... because my teeth get stained with the nicotine. (teeth / clean, it / do)

3. I could hardly speak for almost a week after I .... I had to get another teacher to cover my classes. (wisdom teeth / take out)

4. I'm sure she .... The last time I saw her I remember them sticking out really badly. (ears / pin back)

5. We had been thinking of .... , but we've decided against it for the moment. (the house / redecorate)

6. She had been talking about .... for a while, but I didn't think she'd actually go ahead with it! (tongue / pierce)

7. A: Where .... you .... ?

   B: This place just round the corner. What do you think of it? Do you think I should .... ? (your hair / cut, a bit more / take off)

6 Word building: verbs and adjectives

Complete the sentences with the correct verb or adjective form of the words in brackets.

1. There's a real lack of decent .... housing here. (afford)

2. Plastic surgery is no longer .... in Britain. .... numbers are going under the surgeon's knife. (frown upon, increase)

3. Unfortunately, it's an .... condition. So unless they make a sudden discovery, I'll have it till I die. (cure)

4. He had to undergo .... surgery after the accident because he was so disfigured. (construct)

5. He's a great guy – rich, ... , ... – but unfortunately also .... (create, depend, obtain)

7 Adverbs

Match the adverbs with the group of words they collocate with.

bitterly	internationally	surgically
blissfully	outrageously	uniquely
clinically	socially	
hugely	strictly	

1. .... recognised / renowned / accepted

2. .... unaware / ignorant / happy

3. .... proven / tested / depressed

4. .... removed / inserted / implanted

5. .... dressed / expensive / funny

6. .... confidential / enforced / impartial

7. .... responsible / inclusive / unacceptable

8. .... cold / disappointed / divided

9. .... influential / disappointing / successful

10. .... privileged / qualified / human

8 Expressions with *and*

Complete the sentences with the expressions in the box.

bright and early	now and again	to-ing and fro-ing
cut and dried	pros and cons	touch and go
few and far	sick and tired	trial and error
first and foremost	there and then	tried and tested

1. I decided .... I'd buy it.

2. I was up .... this morning.

3. It's .... whether he'll survive.

4. After some .... the proposal was accepted.

5. We found what works best by ....

6. We're weighing up the .... before we decide.

7. I'm .... of my job.

8. The answer isn't .... It's more complicated.

9. It's a .... method that works.

10. Opportunities to work in the media are .... between.

11. I go swimming .... , but not that often.

12. I'd like to thank everyone, but .... , I'd like to thank my mum.

9 Key words for writing: *indeed*

We use the word *indeed* in several different ways. In written English, it can add a final emphasis after an expression using *very* + certain adjectives and adverbs. It can also introduce a follow-up statement that agrees with a point made beforehand. Look at these examples:

Forecasters predict a very cold winter *indeed*.

The latest edition of Pokora's book is an invaluable reference source for all collectors. *Indeed,* where else could one find such comprehensive descriptions of so many items?

Complete the sentences with the words in the box.

accurately	important	seriously
cautiously	promising	thoroughly
heated	rare	

1. The debate over hunting was very .... indeed.

2. The project is fraught with risk and, as such, we need to proceed very .... indeed.

3. It is very .... indeed that crime prevention measures should be matched by sensitive attention to communities.

4. Things are still at an early stage, but initial results are looking very .... indeed.

5. The government seems to be taking these latest threats very .... indeed.

6. The initial drafts of the contract were checked very .... indeed by our team of lawyers.

7. The vaccination is extremely effective, and adverse reactions would appear to be very .... indeed.

8. The film captures the mood of the times very .... indeed.

Underline the *very* + adjective / adverb + *indeed* expressions in the sentences above.

Language note

In spoken English, we can show we agree with something someone has just said by saying *Indeed*. Look at this example:

A: He's not the most diplomatic person I've ever met.

B: *Indeed!*

Politics and elections

1 | Voting and elections

Complete the sentences with the words in the box.

boycotted	hung	opposition
coalition	landslide	rigging
dictatorship	main	

1. I didn't like the government's policies, so I voted for one of the .... parties.

2. There are three .... parties in our country.

3. The government won the election by a ....

4. The last election resulted in a .... parliament where no-one won an overall majority.

5. The biggest party formed a .... with some of the smaller right-wing parties.

6. The government was accused of .... the election so they would win.

7. One political party .... the election because they didn't think it would be fair.

8. We used to have a .... in our country. Free and fair elections are relatively new.

Now complete these sentences with nouns from the sentences above. Use some nouns more than once.

9. They abandoned the .... they outlined in their manifesto.

10. Iraq had a .... for the best part of 40 years.

11. The government rushed the bill through ....

12. The three-party .... collapsed after a year.

13. The opposition .... is in total disarray.

14. They've called an .... for 8th August.

15. They invaded us and installed a puppet .... !

16. We need more women standing for ....

17. The scandal nearly brought down the ....

2 | It's a fine line

If you say *it's a fine line between* two things, you think there's not much difference between them and it's easy to *cross that line* – move from one thing to the other.

Match the sentence beginnings with the endings.

1. It's a fine line between smooth and ☐
2. It's a fine line between liberator and ☐
3. It's a fine line between genius and ☐
4. It's a fine line between news and ☐
5. It's a fine line between helping and ☐
6. It's a fine line between outbreak and ☐
7. It's a fine line between enough and ☐
8. It's a fine line between fear and ☐

a. propaganda.	d. smarmy.	g. occupier.
b. insanity.	e. exhilaration.	h. interfering.
c. too much.	f. epidemic.	

3 | Talking about politicians

Complete the sentences with the words in the box.

charismatic	flustered	shifty
direct	hypocrite	spark
down-to-earth	passionate	

1. He's got an aura about him. He's very ....

2. He's a real man of the people. He's got no pretensions about him. He seems very ....

3. He comes across as being really .... I mean, he seems to really believe in what he's talking about.

4. He's very straight with people, I'll give him that. He's very .... – always says what he thinks.

5. He never gives a straight answer. He's just really ....

6. He comes across as a bit dull. He hasn't got the .... to get elected.

7. He doesn't practise what he preaches. He's such a .... !

8. He's very smooth. I've never seen him get .... in front of the cameras.

4 Sentences starting with *What*

Rewrite the sentences so that they start with *What* and a verb to emphasise how you feel. The first one has been done as an example.

1. He won't admit to having made mistakes, which is really annoying.
   What really annoys me is the fact that he won't admit to having made mistakes.

2. The lack of investment in education is worrying.

3. They've been ploughing an enormous amount of money into nuclear weapons! It's very disturbing.

4. The guy actually took responsibility for the cock-up and resigned, which was a pleasant change.

5. Proposing to introduce trial without jury is a concern.

6. I know mistakes happen – that's fair enough – but this wasn't an isolated incident. That's the scary thing.

7. He speaks down to people all the time. I get really angry about it.

5 Word building: *elect*

Complete the sentences with the words in the box. You will need to use some words more than once.

elected	elective	re-elected
election	electoral	unelectable
electioneering	electorate	

1. The upcoming general .... promises to be very closely contested.

2. The party is a shambles. They're totally ....

3. There's pressure to reform the ....system.

4. None of the European commissioners are .... , but they wield a lot of power nevertheless.

5. The President needs to appeal to a wider section of the .... if he's going to be .... for a second term.

6. After the disaster, the opposition was accused of .... when they criticised the government's performance. The government said the opposition were exploiting the tragedy for their own .... benefit.

7. The Conservatives suffered their worst .... defeat ever.

8. My wife decided to have an .... caesarean when she had our second child.

6 Collocations

Complete the sentences with the missing collocations from page 50 of the Coursebook.

1. I tried to .... a joke about the situation, but it .... flat.

2. The government only .... 37 per cent of the vote, which isn't exactly a vote of .... in their policies.

3. The meeting to approve the plans to build a new airport was very .... It was repeatedly .... by protesters.

4. In the .... to the .... elections there were allegations that the mayor was trying to .... the election.

5. The government has .... a controversial policy .... at getting people off the dole and into work.

6. The government's stance on immigration has completely .... public opinion. They've even admitted that there are .... of opinion in the cabinet.

7 *Stance on*

Complete the sentences with these words.

abortion	education	pensions
drugs	foreign policy	

1. Their stance on .... is a bit confused. First they want to introduce a national curriculum, and then they want to increase parental choice regarding school selection.

2. I like their stance on .... They want to extend the retirement age and force companies to make higher contributions.

3. Their stance on .... seems far too liberal. I think it should be banned.

4. They take a hard line on .... , which I approve of. They want to toughen the law and increase prison sentences for possession.

5. I'm dead against their stance on .... It's very isolationist. They want to withdraw from various international agreements, put up trade barriers and become more inward-looking.

Find examples of these kinds of collocations:

verb–noun   adjective–noun   noun–noun

Writing: Essay introductions

1 Sample introductions

Complete the paragraphs with the words in the box.

address	pose	unthinkable
becoming	seen	vast
concerned	sinister	whether

Paragraph A

The last five years have [1] ... a massive increase in the use of mobile phones. The [2] ... majority of the population now carry a mobile, whether for work, personal use or emergencies. For most, the idea of returning to a pre-mobile age is [3] ... . However, there may be a more [4] ... side to the explosion in popularity of the mobile phone. Phones may well [5] ... serious health risks, and come with other dangers attached. Let us move on to consider these issues in more detail.

Paragraph B

What we eat is [6] ... more and more newsworthy every day. The daily papers bombard us with a giddy range of celebrity-endorsed diets; bookshops sell recipes to help us lose weight, combat high blood pressure and cholesterol; and experts regularly warn us of the dangers of eating (or not eating) eggs, poultry, fish, red meat, sugar, salt, and so on. In this essay, I intend to [7] ... the pressing questions of [8] ... our obsession with food has escalated out of all proportion, and whether we are right to be [9] ... about the diets that will influence the health of the next generation.

2 Prepositions

Complete the sentences with a preposition in each space.

1. For those in power, the idea .... unlimited access to all manner of information is a threatening one.

2. There has been a significant increase .... the standard of living in the UK.

3. It is perhaps a result of TV overkill that many of us have become desensitised .... the effects of war.

4. The influence of the humanists in Britain has been .... of all proportion to their real number.

5. There has been great concern .... recent proposals for education reform.

6. Whilst many remain unfamiliar .... the emerging nations of Central Asia, they are nevertheless becoming a force to be reckoned with.

7. Whilst these innovations have generally been beneficial, there nevertheless remains a more sinister side .... them.

8. This issue is worth exploring .... more detail.

3 Discussing trends and issues

Cross out the ONE word or expression in italics which does NOT go with the words that follow.

1. There has been *an increasing* / *a phenomenal* / *a steady* rise in the number of racially motivated crimes.

2. There has been *a worrying* / *a growing* / *an alarming* increase in criminal negligence claims.

3. It is often *claimed* / *suggested* / *quoted* that the welfare state is unsustainable in its present form.

4. The *thought* / *notion* / *idea* of part-privatisation is often put forward as being the solution to the problem.

5. However, most previous research in this field has *not concerned* / *failed to consider* / *disregarded* the possibility of terrorist attacks on nuclear power stations.

6. My *aim* / *intent* / *goal* is to show that any decision must be deferred until further research has been undertaken.

4 Writing an introductory paragraph

'We live in an age in which our obsession with celebrity is becoming increasingly harmful.' Discuss.

Write an introductory paragraph. Think about:

• how you are going to highlight the trend

• what further evidence of the trend you could show, or what causes and / or results you want to focus on

• the questions you aim to answer in the essay

Grammar: Continuous forms

1 Tenses

Complete the sentences with the correct continuous form of the verbs in brackets.

1. I .... to grow a beard for the last few weeks, but without much luck so far! I can't believe how long it .... ! (try, take)

2. I .... here for almost 15 years by the time I step down next July. (work)

3. I'm not really sure what was up, but you could see she .... I mean, her eyes were all red and everything. (cry)

4. She .... forever .... my stuff. She goes through my drawers, reads my notes and whenever I ask her what she .... , she just says she ....
(go through, do, clean up)

5. Come this April, I .... here in Japan for eight years all in all. (live)

6. Don't take any notice. He .... just .... silly! (be)

7. There you are! I .... for you for ages! (wait)

8. I .... just .... there, ... my own business when this guy came up and started screaming at me! (stand, mind)

9. A: So what happened? Why did you crash?

   B: Well, it .... for days and when I left the house it .... just .... to snow, so the roads were really treacherous. Anyway, I .... only .... about 30, but I skidded and went off the road into a ditch.
   (rain, start, do)

2 Idioms

Make eight idioms with continuous tenses by putting the words into the correct order.

1. what / you're / said / I / twisting

2. driving / bend / me / it's / the / round

3. tearing / out / been / my / I've / hair

4. throwing / always / around / he's / his / weight

5. our / gaining / we're / on / competitors / ground

6. just / bit / weather / I'm / under / a / feeling / the

7. above / heads / keeping / water / we're / our / just

3 Other continuous forms

Complete the sentences with the verbs in the box in the correct continuous form.

eavesdrop	leak	try	work
go	sit	use	worry

1. I'm afraid the pipe seems to .... for quite some time.

2. Ugh! This cheese must .... in the fridge for months!

3. We've just got to focus on our own strengths and weaknesses. We can't .... about the competition all the time.

4. Listen, I'd better go. I shouldn't really .... the office phone to call you. And anyway, I'm supposed to .... , really!

5. He does finally seem to .... to cut down on how much junk he eats.

6. I'm sorry you heard what I said, but you shouldn't .... on our conversation!

7. He couldn't .... that fast when he crashed. Otherwise, the car would've been a total write-off.

4 Simple or continuous?

Choose the correct form.

1. I've *been going / gone* to Malta for my summer holidays for years now.

2. I *hadn't been enjoying / hadn't enjoyed* work for quite some time, so in the end, I *was just deciding / just decided* to pack it in.

3. He actually had the nerve to ask me if I've *been seeing / seen* another man! And I thought he *was trusting / trusted* me!

4. *I'd been toying / I'd toyed* with the idea of starting my own blog for ages, and then I *was doing / did* this computer course and that really *was helping / helped* me get things together.

5. I've *been having / had* the exact same problem as you more times than I care to remember!

6. It's strange that you should call now! I *was actually just thinking of / actually just thought of* ringing you.

7. This is the first time I've *been trying / tried* Thai food.

The weather and the environment

1 Describing the weather

Complete the texts with the words in the boxes.

chill	corner	glorious	topping	turned

It's mid-October, but we're in the middle of an Indian summer. The weather here has been absolutely (1) ... all month – the days are dry and bright, with temperatures sometimes (2) ... 20 degrees. The leaves on the trees have all (3) ... golden brown and the evenings are cool, but not cold. There's a slight (4) ... in the air early morning and there's been some mist, but otherwise you could easily forget that winter is just round the (5) ... !

bucketed down	hailstorm	scorching
dire	humidity	torrential
fog	muggy	unbearable
gale	pig	

Had a miserable time in Blackpool. The weather was absolutely (6) ... ! It (7) ... non-stop for three days and it blew up a (8) ... one day. The sky was so overcast most days that we didn't see the sun, and most nights a thick freezing (9) ... came sweeping in from the sea. You won't be surprised to hear we hardly ventured out of our B&B. We did try to go out for a walk one night – but ended up getting caught in a (10) ... !

But we're in Singapore now and it's absolutely (11) ... . Honestly, the heat is almost (12) ... . It's in the high eighties most of the time, but the real problem is the (13) ... . I've been sweating like a (14) ... since we arrived. It's so (15) ... and close that it's hard to breathe! The locals tell me that the rainy season is just round the corner, and that when the rains start, they're usually absolutely (16) ....

2 Common similes

Match the sentence beginnings with the endings.

1. It was complete chaos! We were all running around ☐
2. It'll be sold out soon. Tickets have been selling ☐
3. It's an amazing city! The people there party ☐
4. Who does he think he is, walking around ☐
5. His room was a complete tip. Honestly, it looked ☐
6. Trying to track down my stolen bike is ☐
7. She's taken to her new school ☐
8. You can criticise him as much as you like. It won't make any difference to him. It's ☐

a. like water off a duck's back.
b. like trying to find a needle in a haystack.
c. like he owns the place?   d. like hot cakes.
e. like there's no tomorrow.   f. ike headless chickens.
g. like a duck to water.   h. like a bomb had hit it!

3 *Not* + negative adjectives

Complete the sentences with these adjectives.

dissimilar	unexpected	unlike
impossible	unhappy	unusual

1. It could be quite difficult, but it's not ....
2. Nowadays it's not .... for a woman in the UK to keep her own surname when she marries, rather than take her husband's.
3. He passed away last year. Mind you, he was 89, so it wasn't ....
4. It's a great game. It's not .... Tetris really.
5. There are obviously differences, but Rome is not that .... to London in lots of ways.
6. It's not ideal, but I'm not .... about it.

Language note

This means it's 'raining very heavily'. People also say it's *pissing down*, but some think this is rude and don't use it.

4 Noun phrases

Complete the sentences with these nouns.

bullets	complaints	information	suspicion
change	depression	protest	~~time~~

1. The origins of the dance have been <u>lost in the mists of _time_</u>, but it is still performed in some rural areas.

2. The TV company received a flood of .... because of the explicit sex and violence in the programme.

3. The riots were basically sparked by the police killing this guy in a hail of .... in broad daylight.

4. I did some research into it on the Web, but I ended up buried beneath an avalanche of .... !

5. It's been a one-party state for years, but it looks like the winds of .... have started blowing.

6. For now, the President has escaped legal action, but a cloud of .... still hangs over him.

7. I just felt really low. It was as if I'd spend the rest of my days living under a cloud of ....

8. The film's release was greeted by a storm of .... , with demonstrations being held and thousands calling for it to be banned.

Now underline the noun phrase and the verb that goes with it in each sentence.

5 Weather idioms

Choose the correct word.

1. I'm feeling a bit under the _clouds / weather_.

2. My dad sat up waiting for my sister till three in the morning – and then she came _breezing / blowing_ in like nothing had happened!

3. I can't believe I ended up trying to kiss him! All the wine must've _clouded / fogged_ my judgement!

4. There were all these rumours going round about him, so he left under a bit of a _storm / cloud_.

5. I was quite nervous before I met her family, but they gave me a really _warm / hot_ welcome.

6. I'm totally snowed _in / under_ with work at the moment!

7. We had a big row and he got so angry he just _poured / stormed_ out. I haven't seen him since!

8. Robinho got a very _frosty / frozen_ reception from the crowd when he played against his old club.

6 Weather conversations

Complete the conversations with the pairs of words in the box.

chilly + bitter	rain + spitting
downpour + soaked	raining + pissing
draught + heating	stuffy + sauna
forecast + miserable	weird + warming

1. A: Is it still .... outside?
   B: Yeah, it's .... down.

2. A: Was that .... ?
   B: Yeah, it's just started ....

3. A: Did you get caught in that .... earlier?
   B: Yeah, I got absolutely .... !

4. A: .... today, isn't it?
   B: Yeah, ... !

5. A: This is such .... weather.
   B: I know, it's so mild! It's global .... !

6. A: Can I open the window? It's so ....
   B: Yeah, go ahead. It's like a .... , isn't it?

7. A: What's the .... for tomorrow?
   B: Absolutely .... – and no sign of it brightening up!

8. A: Can I close the door? I'm caught in the ....
   B: Yes, sure. Shall I stick the .... on too?

7 Word building

Complete the collocations with the correct form of the words given.

1. **environment**
   a leading .... , ... aware

2. **commerce**
   not .... viable, a .... success

3. **assume**
   make a false .... , ... you're right

4. **subsidy**
   heavily .... , end .... of healthcare

5. **renew**
   use more .... energy, show .... interest

6. **destroy**
   save it from .... , have a .... effect

7. **permit**
   grant planning .... , a very .... society

8. **consume**
   reduce .... , meet the needs of ....

8 The greenhouse effect

Complete the text with ONE word in each space.

The greenhouse effect

If you believe what you read in the papers, there is little (1) ... that the greenhouse (2) ... on the earth is becoming stronger. However, it seems there is (3) ... certainty about the results of this change. On the one (4) ... , we see stories that increases in sea temperatures and the depletion of the ozone (5) ... will lead to the ice (6) ... melting and sea levels rising. This may contaminate fresh water supplies; it may flood beaches, which cannot move back because of human construction and buildings; and in some cases, it may even threaten the (7) ... existence of low-lying islands. Yet it is also argued by some that these same processes may lead to the Gulf Stream (the warm sea currents that stop the UK and other parts of Europe from freezing) slowing down or switching off completely. The result of this would be sharp drops in temperature akin (8) ... a new ice age. This is a (9) ... cry from other stories which say that global warming will bring droughts to southern Europe (10) ... the north will bask in a Mediterranean climate, allowing Britons to grow olive trees and grape vines.

Perhaps we should just ignore all this speculation and (11) ... on the real environmental crises that are affecting us right now. Sulphurous emissions continue to cause acid (12) ... , which destroys forests. The deforestation of huge tracts of land has led to erosion and flooding. This is (13) ... to the fact that water can now run off the land. Intensive farming has led to desertification, the most (14) ... example of which is the Aral Sea in Uzbekistan. The rivers that fed the sea were diverted to irrigate the land in (15) ... to grow cotton. Over the years, the waters of what was once the world's fourth largest inland sea have receded to the (16) ... of a large lake, leaving toxic residues and salt which are blown over the land, (17) ... contamination and disease. Cancer and tuberculosis are rife in the area. Such devastation has little to (18) ... with global warming and was entirely avoidable.

Language note

(their) very existence: We often use *very* as an adjective to emphasise how important/extreme something is.
akin to: This means 'similar to something else'.

9 Key words for writing: reference

There are several ways to refer back to a previous point or item of correspondence. Some of these expressions are similar and easily confused. For example:

I am writing *regarding* the complaint you made to our customer services department.

I am writing *with regard to* the complaint you made to our customer services department.

Complete the sentences with these words.

refer	regarding	respect

1. We wish to talk to you .... your personal use of the office PC.

2. With .... to your recent claim, I am afraid we are unable to progress without further details being supplied.

3. I .... to your letter of 5th May, in which you requested details of the payments made to your account.

Match these sentence beginnings with the endings.

4. With reference to your recent application, ☐
5. The head teacher would like to talk to you concerning ☐
6. I refer to your comments ☐
7. With regard to your continued absence from work, ☐
8. Re where to meet tonight, ☐

a. in your e-mail dated 7th July.
b. we shall unfortunately have to terminate your contract.
c. your son's behaviour in class.
d. would you please let us have the names of two referees?
e. I'd suggest that Italian place in Brook Street.

Complete the sentences with these prepositions.

of	to	to	with

9. I refer .... your recent letter.
10. I am contacting you .... respect to your enquiry.
11. You mentioned this in your letter .... 8th June.
12. I am writing with regard .... your recent enquiry.

10 Shopping

1 Collocations

Match the verbs with the noun phrases they collocate with.

cast	drain	remain	undercut
claim	introduce	smuggle	
dent	launch	uncover	

1. .... drugs / people into the country
2. .... my faith / profits / my confidence
3. .... social security / it on insurance
4. .... a terrorist plot / a web of corruption
5. .... light on the issue / doubt on the theory
6. .... a crackdown on piracy / an attack
7. .... buoyant / sluggish / successful
8. .... resources / a lake / me emotionally
9. .... your competitors' prices / local shops
10. .... stiffer penalties / new draconian legislation

2 Word building: phrasal verb nouns

Complete the sentences with nouns made from the verbs in the box.

| break down | hand over | pass by |
| bring up | lay out | walk out |

1. Your new website's great! I love the .... !
2. I was in Hong Kong in 1997, during the ....
3. He was under so much pressure at work that he ended up having a nervous ....
4. The union led a .... in protest at the sackings.
5. This guy tried to attack me in the street. Luckily, though, this .... intervened and saved me!
6. I was brought up by my grandparents, and looking back on it, I guess it was a fairly unconventional ....

Learning tip

There is no reason why some compound nouns are written as one word and others are hyphenated. You just have to try and remember the way the nouns are written.

3 Water metaphors and idioms (1)

Complete the text with the words in the box.

| drop | floodgates | trickle |
| flood | stream | wave |

The words we use to talk about the movement of water are also used to talk about the quantity and movement of other things. For example, if we think that an amount of money is very small and not nearly big enough to deal with a problem, we can say (1) *it's a* .... *in the ocean.* When people are moving slowly from one place to another, we talk about (2) *a* .... *of people;* when the numbers and the speed increase, it becomes (3) *a steady* .... *of people* and when there are large numbers of people moving quickly, it's (4) *a* .... *of people.* If a government changes the law to make it much easier for things or people to move, they (5) *open the* .... This sometimes has a negative connotation. Indeed, it might provoke (6) *a* .... *of anger and protest* from people opposed to immigration!

4 Water metaphors and idioms (2)

Make eight common water idioms by matching the sentence beginnings with the endings.

1. During the recession, many smaller firms went ☐
2. On my wages it's a real struggle to keep ☐
3. That row was years ago. It's all water ☐
4. I didn't get any training. They just threw me in ☐
5. I didn't get any help at all. I was just left to sink ☐
6. I think his comments landed him ☐
7. I guess I'm your typical floating ☐
8. Someone inside the government leaked ☐

a. the news to the press.
b. my head above water.
c. under the bridge now.
d. or swim.
e. at the deep end.
f. voter.
g. under.
h. in hot water with the boss!

5 Don't you think ... ?

Complete the conversations with the pairs of words in the box.

loud + bright	frumpy + gran
clash + place	revealing + imagination
extravagant + splash out	stumpy + slender
flimsy + sturdy	tacky + nasty

1. A: You don't think it's a bit .... ?

   B: It doesn't look that .... It'll probably collapse with any weight on it.

2. A: You don't think it's a bit too .... ?

   B: Well, it doesn't leave much to the .... !

3. A: I quite like this one. It's really warm. You don't think it's a bit .... ?

   B: To be brutally honest, you look like my .... !

4. A: You don't think it's a bit .... ?

   B: If you really want my honest opinion, yes, it just looks incredibly cheap and .... !

5. A: You don't think they make my legs look .... ?

   B: No! I wish mine were as .... as yours!

6. A: You don't think they're a bit .... ?

   B: I can't say I'd spend that much on jewellery myself, but hey, why not .... ?

7. A: You don't think it's a bit .... ?

   B: No, those big .... patterns suit you.

8. A: You don't think it'll .... with the other furniture?

   B: No. It wouldn't look out of .... in your house. And anyway, that mixed kind of style is in at the moment.

Match the things in the box with the conversations above.

birthday card	tight jeans	table
lamp	dangly earrings	flowery shirt
cardigan	skimpy dress	

6 Idioms

Make idioms by putting the words in order. Then translate the idioms into your language.

1. the / the / tip / it's / iceberg / of
2. final / was / it / straw / the
3. blind / turn / they / eye / to / a / it
4. few / ideas / a / have / the / eyebrows / raised
5. yourself / put / in / shoes / their
6. been / feet / off / my / I've / rushed
7. my / the / is / down / boss / neck / breathing
8. a / shoulders / huge / it's / weight / my / off

7 Clothes and jewellery

Translate these words into your own language.

baggy	flared	lapel	polo-neck
buckle	flat	paisley	seams
collar	flip-flops	pinstripe	sleeve
cuff	hood	pleated	tartan
dangly	knee-length	polka dots	tassled

8 Problems with clothes and things

Complete each pair of sentences with a word in the box in the correct form.

chip	crack	fray	rip
compatible	fall apart	fuzzy	shrink

1a. It wasn't .... with my system.

1b. They split up because they weren't ....

2a. The T-shirt .... in the wash.

2b. The economy's .... as we're in recession.

3a. When I got it home, I realised there was a hairline .... in the cup.

3b. .... are beginning to appear in the coalition.

4a. The picture was just really ....

4b. My memory's a bit .... about what happened.

5a. When I got back, I found the sleeve was ....

5b. Their defence was just .... apart by the prosecuting lawyers.

6a. My shoes are already ....

6b. He was well up in the last set, but then his game ....

7a. I got the jeans second-hand, so they were a bit .... at the edges.

7b. We were so tired and working under such pressure that tempers did begin to ....

8a. When I got back, I realised the plate was ....

8b. We're slowly .... away at their market dominance.

Writing: Letters of complaint

1 | Sample letter

Complete the letter with the words in the box.

addition	attention	concerning	surely
alternative	cite	speaking	unaware

Dear Sir/Madam,

I live adjacent to your school in Grasmere Road and I am writing regarding the atrocious behaviour of some of your younger students. In (1) ... to this, I should like to bring to your (2) ... the irresponsibility of certain members of your staff when supervising students' evening activities.

Firstly, (3) ... the students' behaviour, I should like you to make it very clear to those students walking along Grasmere Road towards the station that my front garden is not a rubbish dump. When they leave school in the afternoons, they pass my house and dispose of empty cans, chocolate wrappers and even cigarette packets (although most of them are below the age for smoking) on my grass.

Could you also please ask your students not to shout and use bad language in the street, as this is detrimental to the reputation of both your school and the area?

Regarding certain members of your staff, you are perhaps (4) ... of the fact that the evening activities sometimes continue well beyond ten and the noise is excessive. I (5) ... as an example last Thursday night when the noise did not stop until 10.30 pm. (6) ... the members of staff supervising these activities could bring the events to a close at a reasonable hour.

I know that I am (7) ... for many households in the locality when I ask you to speak to your students and staff about these matters.

Should they continue to be so inconsiderate, I shall be forced to take matters further and shall have no (8) ... but to contact the council.

Yours faithfully, Mrs J Barker

2 | Being diplomatic

When we want to make a complaint sound softer and allow the recipient to save face, we often 'hedge' things. Look at these examples:

Perhaps you are *unaware of* the effect of your actions on the local community.

Perhaps you are *unaware of the fact that* your actions have had a detrimental effect on the local community.

Complete the sentences with *of* or *of the fact that*.

1. Perhaps you are unaware .... people are losing a great deal of money in this venture.

2. Perhaps you are unaware .... the problems caused by bullying in schools.

3. You are perhaps unaware .... I have been waiting six months for a reply.

4. Perhaps you are unaware .... your chef has no qualifications whatsoever.

5. You are perhaps unaware .... the damage which is caused to your reputation by allowing such behaviour to continue.

6. Perhaps you are unaware .... the reasons for the decision to lay staff off.

Match these follow-up comments to the sentences above.

a. I suggest you take up references in future when employing staff.

b. As such, I would obviously appreciate a response in the very near future.

c. Indeed, several investors are now on the verge of bankruptcy.

d. Word of mouth is a powerful tool, and could go on to do your firm great harm.

e. The school has lost money and cuts must be made.

f. Left unchecked, it can scar victims for life.

3 | Practice

Imagine you are a student at the school. Write a letter to your local newspaper complaining about a problem near your house or school. Decide:

• what the problem is

• what you would like done about it

• what you are going to do if nothing is done

Next, plan the content of each paragraph. Then write the letter.

11 | Relationships

1 Relationship phrasal verbs

Complete the sentences with the correct form of the phrasal verbs in the box.

bring up	get through to	rub up
fall out	make up	show off
get away with	pick on	

1. When I was 17, I .... with my brother over a girl we both fancied! It was years before we .... and started properly talking again!

2. I don't get on with my cousin. I'm not sure why. We just seem to .... each other .... the wrong way.

3. My big brother always used to .... me when we were growing up! He made my life hell!

4. She's an only child and she's always .... ! She's always got to be the centre of attention.

5. I was .... to believe that I was no better or no worse than anybody else.

6. My mum really used to dote on my little brother. Honestly, she used to let him .... murder.

7. I've tried talking to my son about how important his studies are, but I just can't .... him.

2 Word building: phrasal verb nouns

Complete the sentences with these nouns.

breakup	falling-out	send-off
come-on	get-together	show-off
dropout	hang-ups	

1. They had a big .... a few years ago – and haven't spoken to each other since!

2. We don't see each other that much, but we usually have a big family .... every Christmas.

3. He's a right .... – a real attention seeker!

4. She's a .... She's never had a proper job.

5. She's leaving the company next week. We're going to give her a good .... when she goes.

6. The .... of his marriage sent him off the rails.

7. She's quite neurotic. She has a lot of ....

8. He was being flirty and giving me the .... !

3 Must / might / can't

Choose the correct form.

1. A: I honestly thought we were all goners.
   B: God, that *must / might* have been terrifying.

2. A: We were snowed in for nearly four days.
   B: Really? That *can't / mustn't* have been much fun.

3. A: I don't know why she got in such a strop.
   B: Well, it *might / can't* have had something to do with the fact you kept making fun of her accent!

4. He *can't / might not* be coming. He would've been here by now otherwise.

5. He must *have done / have been doing* at least a hundred when he crashed.

6. Tatiana just phoned to say she's not coming. I guess she can't *be feeling / feel* very well.

7. If I hadn't met her when I did, things *might have / might have been* worked out very differently.

8. She *can't have seen / can't have been seeing* us. She would've come over and said hello otherwise.

4 Complete and utter

Complete the sentences with *complete and utter* + a noun.

bore	disregard	mess
breakdown	failure	waste
disgrace	lack	

1. It's a .... of my time and his parents' money trying to teach him anything! He just shows .... of interest.

2. I was a .... at school. I left when I was 16.

3. He just shows a .... for any of my feelings.

4. The decision to acquit him was a .... He was obviously guilty.

5. The whole project is in a .... There's no leadership.

6. There has been a .... of law and order.

7. The guy's a .... , the way he rambles on all the time.

5 Keyword: *suppose*

Find nine sentences with *suppose*. Mark the end of each sentence using /. Translate the sentences into your own language.

supposehewashavinganaffairwhatwouldyoudothenwhat'sthat

supposedtomeanhowwasIsupposedtoknowthey'reOK I

supposebutthey'renotmyfavouritebandI'msupposedtobegoing

outbutIcouldgetoutofitit'ssupposedtobebrilliantIwassupposed

tomeethimlastweekbuthecancelledIdon'tsupposeyoucould

givemealiftcouldyouIsupposeso

Complete the conversations with seven of the sentences from above.

1. A: He said I should 'consider my position'.
   B: .... ? Is that a threat or what?

2. A: What're you up to later?
   B: .... What did you have in mind?

3. A: I love Tim Burton's films.
   B: Me too. Have you seen his latest?
   ....

4. A: Are you sure you want to stay with him?
   .... ?
   B: Don't know. Dump him probably. It depends.

5. A: You really put your foot in it with Ruth.
   B: Well, ... she'd split up with Darren?

6. A: I'm late for my meeting.
   .... ?
   B: .... I'm not exactly rushed off my feet. Let me just get the keys.

6 Annoying habits

Match the verbs with the words they go with.

1. hog ☐   a. me while I'm talking
2. barge in ☐   b. the bathroom for hours
3. interrupt ☐   c. fault with everything I do
4. find ☐   d. without knocking
5. put ☐   e. assumptions about me
6. eavesdrop ☐   f. my head off
7. follow ☐   g. on my conversations
8. take ☐   h. words in my mouth
9. leave ☐   i. the mickey
10. make ☐   j. about how awful his life is
11. go on ☐   k. me around all the time
12. bite ☐   l. his papers lying around

7 Expressing annoyance

Using the ideas below, write complete sentences to complain about a flatmate.

1. I wish he / clear up / once / while
2. all he / sit / backside all day / play on his PlayStation
3. he / always / eavesdrop / my conversations
4. I wish he / the mickey / my English / the time
5. I wish he / knock / before / barge into / my room
6. he / exactly / considerate / ever met
7. he / constantly / his things / lie around
8. he / exactly / go out of his way / be helpful

8 Describing feelings

Complete the sentences with the pairs of words in the box.

collected + unflappable	lost + tongue-tied
devastated + broke down	mortified + swallow
embarrassed + went	pissed off + bugged
livid + rage	stiff + fear

1. I was scared .... I was literally shaking with ....

2. I was absolutely .... when I heard he'd died. I just .... and cried.

3. I was so .... when it happened. I .... bright red!

4. What he said was out of order! I was .... about it. It really .... me!

5. I was .... Honestly, I wanted the ground to open up and .... me whole!

6. We were running round like headless chickens, but she was her usual self – cool, calm and .... She's totally ....

7. He usually keeps his cool, but this time he was just .... ! He was shaking with ....

8. It's not often I'm .... for words, but I did get a bit .... when I tried to talk to him.

Language note

If someone is *pissed off*, they are very annoyed. Some people find it offensive to use the word *piss*, and it's best not to use it with older people or with people you don't know that well.

Don't confuse *He's pissed off* with *He's pissed*, which in British English means 'He's drunk' or *Piss off* which means 'Go away' or 'Get lost'.

9 Reporting conversations

Complete the sentences by putting the words in brackets in the correct order.

1. I think we'd just got off on the wrong foot, but .... (heart / we / of / a / heart / bit / to / a / had) and things have been a lot better since.

2. I think her parents were a bit wary of me when we arrived, but .... (win / over / to / I / them / managed) during the course of the evening.

3. .... (the / take / way / this / don't / wrong), but how long have you two been seeing each other?

4. I was worried about the results and I'm afraid .... (the / fears / worst / my / doctor / confirmed).

5. I don't mind a bit of criticism, but .... (just / he / on / about / on / went / and / it).

6. I must've told him a thousand times not to leave the door unlocked, but .... (wall / it / like / talking / a / is / brick / to). He never listens to a word I say!

7. I tried to explain I'd done nothing wrong and that it was all a big misunderstanding, but .... (of / having / she / was / it / none). In fact, she said I could go to hell!

10 *Not exactly*

Complete the sentences with *not exactly* and the correct form of the words in brackets.

1. A: What did you think of the film?
   B: Well, it .... (Shakespeare), but I guess it was entertaining enough.

2. A: I've never heard of this band before.
   B: No? Well, they .... (set) the world alight so far, but a couple of their tracks are OK.

3. A: How was your evening?
   B: Well, having dinner with my parents-in-law .... (my idea / night out), but all things considered it was OK.

4. A: Why don't you want to go in the car?
   B: Well, put it this way, you .... (safe / driver / world) and I'd rather get there in one piece!

11 Key words for writing: conditional links

There are many other ways we can convey conditionality, apart from using *if* and *unless*. Look at these examples:

Assuming (that) nothing is done to combat global warming, the next generation will face serious environmental problems.

Provided (that) we have a mild winter, most gas bills should not be too high.

On the condition that you can start work immediately, we would like to offer you the position.

Providing (that) your son continues to work hard, he should do well in his exams.

Correct the mistake in each of the sentences.

1. With the condition that we receive the contract by the end of the week, we shall be able to commence work on 15th May.

2. Assuming the condition that everyone agrees with the amendments, I will give the plan the go-ahead.

3. Provide that his work is up to standard, there will be no need for further action.

4. The company says it will accept the wage demands on the assuming that the union accepts job cuts.

Match these sentence beginnings with the endings.

5. He has been released ☐
6. We should be able to make a decision later today ☐
7. You will be allowed to take the case on the plane ☐
8. Your teeth should remain in good condition ☐

a. provided that it is not too large.
b. on the condition that he reports to the police station every day.
c. assuming that we have all the relevant information.
d. if you have regular check-ups.

Join these sentences using the words in brackets. Make any other necessary changes.

9. These books are lent to students. They must return them within three days. (on the condition that)

10. The competition should raise £1,000. Everyone is expected to donate at least £50. (assuming)

11. The meeting should finish at 2.45. People have been asked to arrive at 1.30. (provided that)

12. Parcels will arrive in time for Christmas. People should post them before 10th December. (providing)

12 Economics and finance

1 Talking about the economy

Complete the sentences with the words in the box.

booming	colossal	recession
bottoming out	mess	tiger
collapsed	miracle	turnaround

1. At the start of the 90s, the economy completely
   .... There was rampant inflation and the
   country ended up being saddled with ....
   debts.

2. The economy is .... at the moment. New
   businesses are springing up all over the place. It's
   the new .... economy in the region.

3. After the economic .... of the 80s, the
   economy went into .... – and has
   remained there pretty much ever since!

4. The economy's been on a downward spiral for a
   year, so signs that the recession's finally
   .... are welcome.

5. When the government came to power, the
   economy was a complete .... , but
   there's been a bit of a .... over the last
   year or so, and things are starting to look up.

Now complete these sentences with the words in the box.

bust	picked up	rocketed
foundations	reforms	slowdown
peaked	rock	wall

6. After the economy hit .... bottom in 2001,
   things .... a bit, with GDP increasing about
   3 per cent per year since then.

7. The economy seems to be stuck in a bit of a boom
   .... cycle.

8. The last government pushed through a series of
   .... which laid the .... for economic
   growth.

9. All the signs are that the economy has ....
   and that a gradual .... will follow.

10. Loads of small businesses have gone to the
    .... over the last few years.
    Unemployment has ....

2 Word building

Complete the sentences with the correct form of the word *economy*.

1. I studied .... at Liverpool University.

2. It's a tight budget, so we're going to have to
   .... if we're going to stay within it and not
   overspend.

3. He's one of the world's leading ....

4. I just don't think the project is .... viable.

5. I didn't call you a liar! I just said I think you've been a
   bit .... with the truth!

6. The factory was .... , so they closed it
   down.

7. Their .... policies have made things worse.

3 Voicing your opinion

Complete the sentences with ONE word in each space.

1. I'm a big .... of the idea of capping the
   number of hours you're allowed to work.

2. To be honest, I don't really know where I
   .... on the whole issue of the Euro.

3. I'm very much in .... of banning smoking.

4. It's a great idea in .... , but I just can't see
   it working in practice.

5. I'm fundamentally .... to the whole notion
   of marriage!

6. I'm not really sure what I think about the new laws.
   I'm still in two .... about it all, really.

7. I fully .... the idea of part-privatisation of
   the NHS. It'll bring in much needed finance.

8. I've got grave .... about the economic
   viability of the plan. I just can't see it working.

Language note

If you're *still in two minds about* an issue and *can't
decide where you stand on* it, people might get annoyed
with you and tell you to *stop sitting on the fence,* or ask
you to *get off the fence.* You need to *decide which side
of the fence you're on* – if you're *pro* or *anti* an idea.

4 | Adjective–noun collocations

Match the adjectives with the nouns they collocate with.

bright	draconian	grave
crippling	drastic	tight
dismal	dwindling	

1. .... measures / action / cutbacks
2. .... budget / deadline / schedule / squeeze
3. .... disease / debt / injury / taxes
4. .... results / weather / performance
5. .... situation / error / reservations
6. .... legislation / conditions / rules
7. .... resources / sales / hopes / population
8. .... future / clothes / weather / idea

5 | The history of a business

Complete the story with ONE word in each space.

I (1) .... up an Internet-based travel company in the late 90s using my savings. I also took (2) .... a loan and raised another £50,000 (3) .... a venture capitalist in return (4) .... a 30 per cent stake in the business. The company struggled for a couple of years, recording big (5) .... , but as the Internet spread our company took off. Although we still weren't (6) .... even, we made big increases in sales.

We decided to diversify and in order to raise more capital, we floated on the (7) .... exchange. The share (8) .... immediately rocketed. However, the bubble soon (9) .... and our share price slumped. In 2004, there was a (10) .... bid from one of our rival companies. Although I was personally (11) .... the bid, the board (12) .... the offer to the shareholders.

6 | *Best / better / worst*

Complete the sentences by putting the words in brackets in order.

1. Personally, I think running a business from home is actually .... (worlds / worst / all / the / of). No home life, longer hours and no security. .... (off / I / been / have / better / would) staying with my old company.

2. Business is .... (best / times / of / the / difficult / at), but now it's impossible.

3. Business was booming, but since January .... (turn / worse / taken / for / have / a / the / things).

4. I know it's not good, but .... (make / just / bad / to / job / the / have / of / a / we'll / best).

5. .... (best / part / I / the / of / spent / ten / years) in teaching before I decided to go into business.

6. I know it's not a big pay rise, but .... (than / kick / the / better / a / it's / in / teeth).

7. Since the companies merged, ... (changed / the / things / definitely / for / have / better).

8. I am a bit short of money, but .... (worst / the / the / comes / to / if / worst) I could always sell my car.

7 | Debt collocations

Complete the paragraphs with the words in the box.

burden	crippling	outstanding	settle
cleared	got into	ran up	stand
collector	incur	restructure	write off

1. As many Third World countries are struggling under the .... of debt, there is pressure on western governments to simply .... the debts. In some cases, the interest the debts .... is actually greater than the country's entire budget for health and education.

2. The football club has been brought to the brink of bankruptcy thanks to .... debts and poor results. Even after the sale of its star assets, the debts .... at over £70 million. The club is meeting creditors to .... its debts.

3. I first .... debt when I lost my job. I didn't make the adjustments to my lifestyle that I needed to and .... a huge debt on my credit card. I .... the credit card debt by taking out a bank loan, but then I fell behind on my repayments. When I refused to .... the debt, the bank sent round a debt .... to seize furniture and assets to pay for what was ....

Writing: Anecdotes

1 | Sample anecdote

Complete the anecdote with the words in the box.

about	direction	fate	straight
blame	due	finally	worse
burst	eavesdropping	happen	

Twice removed!

Ever had a bad journey? Well, it can't have been much (1) .... than a story I overheard on the tube the other day. I wasn't actually (2) .... , but when you're squashed up against commuters in the rush hour it's difficult to avoid listening in.

It was on the Northern Line last Monday evening. Two women travelling back from a meeting were talking over my head (I'm only 5'1", so it wasn't difficult) about the chair of the meeting, who had rolled in several hours late that morning. Apparently, the poor woman had had that kind of run of bad luck you tend to (3) .... on the stars.

She'd started out well in time for the meeting, which was (4) .... to begin at 9.15, but while changing lines, she'd taken a tumble down the steps leading to the platform. Her briefcase flew ahead of her, (5) .... open and scattered papers in the path of the stampeding commuters, who trampled them underfoot. The unfortunate lady twisted her ankle and laddered her tights. Bad luck, you may say, could (6) .... to anyone. But read on!

Having gathered all her belongings, she hobbles onto the platform as speedily as her ankle will let her, where her train is (7) .... to leave. With a heroic effort, she flings herself into the carriage. Unfortunately, the doors then close and trap her left ankle. When she was (8) .... released by the doors, she now had two damaged ankles, raised blood pressure and was running an hour late.

She got off at the next station, supported by a helpful member of the public, and practically crawled to the platform for her next change. She made it into the tube with no further mishap. However, after a few minutes, she realised that she was travelling in the wrong (9) .... ! An hour later, she finally arrived at the meeting.

I am sure I would have stumbled to a taxi, gone (10) .... home and spent the rest of the day in bed. Who knows what (11) .... would've had in store for the journey home?

2 | Ways of doing things

Complete the sentences with the correct form of the verbs in the box.

gaze	leer	screech	strut
giggle	mumble	smash	trudge
hobble	peer	sprint	whisper

1. Anyway, I .... into the darkness and could just make out this figure.

2. I couldn't believe it! He's my best friend's boyfriend – and he kept .... in my ear during dinner and suggesting all kinds of things!

3. I slipped and bashed my knee on the kerb, and then I had to .... back to the office. It was awful!

4. The glass slipped out of my hand and .... on the floor.

5. I guess it was kind of immature really, but we both started .... like schoolgirls when he said he was with Hotmail!

6. So in the end we had to .... five miles back to the hotel through the sleet and snow. I was almost dead by the time we got there.

7. I felt really uncomfortable because this slimy guy kept .... at me across the room.

8. I .... just .... out of the window thinking about what I was going to do that night and, of course, the teacher asked me a question!

9. Honestly, it was so annoying watching him .... around like he owned the place.

10. I sat next to this weird guy who .... to himself the whole journey.

11. So we .... through the station and managed to jump on to the train as it was pulling out.

12. This car came bombing down the road and .... to a halt right in front of us.

3 | Writing an anecdote

Write an anecdote about a story you once overheard or were told. Before you start writing, choose some language that you want to use from this page and from Writing: Anecdotes and stories in the Coursebook.

Grammar: The future

1 Ways of talking about the future (1)

Choose the more natural form.

1. I can't make it tonight. *I've got to / I'll* work late if I'm going to meet this deadline.

2. I can't wait to go to Greece. It *must / should* be great!

3. Just think. This time next week, I'll *lounge / be lounging* by the pool in the sunshine! I can't wait!

4. *I see / I'll be seeing* Rengin while I'm in Istanbul, so *I'll let / I'll be letting* her know you've moved.

5. We're *going / supposed to be going* to Germany in the summer, but to be honest, I'm not sure if we'll be able to afford it.

6. Look, I can't really talk now. We're *just about to / bound to* go out in a second. *I'll / I'm going to* call you back later on, OK.

7. If they're serious, then they're *going to have to / having to* make a much better offer than that!

8. There's no point denying it. She's *bound to find out / on the verge of finding out* about it sooner or later.

9. The whole country is *on the verge of becoming / due to become* an environmental disaster zone!

10. I've got a few friends *about to come down / coming down* from Scotland next week.

2 Ways of talking about the future (2)

Complete the sentences with the verbs in brackets in the most likely form.

1. A: My plane .... at nine tonight. (leave)

   B: Oh right. Who .... you .... with? (fly)

   A: Emirates.

2. I feel dreadful. I think I .... (be sick)

3. A: What .... you .... later? Any plans? (do)

   B: I .... some friends in town, but I'm wiped out so I might just phone and cancel. (meet)

4. A: Made any New Year's resolutions?

   B: Yeah, I .... and stop smoking ! (try)

5. It's depressing to think that by the time I .... paying off the loan, I .... double what I borrowed. (finish, pay back)

6. I .... a soul about it, I promise. (tell)

3 Ways of talking about the future (3)

There are several ways of talking about the future that use expressions rather than tenses. Look at the patterns that go with these expressions.

The first phase of construction *is due to be* completed in 2015.

You're *bound to feel* a bit culture-shocked when you first arrive.

You can try if you want, but it's *unlikely to make* much difference.

I'm *(just) about to go* insane here, doing this!

They did well in the last election and *are set to do* better next year.

To be honest, I think she's *on the verge of filing* for divorce.

I'm actually *on the point of submitting* my novel to the publishers.

In newspaper headlines, you often see the following pattern:

President *to visit* Pakistan next week.

In newspaper articles, this pattern is also quite common:

The President *is to visit* Pakistan next week.

Rewrite the sentences using the words in bold so that they have similar meanings.

1. It seems probable that the takeover will not be approved. **quite unlikely**
   The takeover ....

2. Record profits are expected to be announced by BT today. **set**
   BT ....

3. A takeover of the firm is now inevitable. **is to**
   The firm ....

4. The whole village is about to be swallowed up by the sea. **on the point of**
   The whole village ....

5. In many parts of the country, there are almost no tigers left. **verge**
   Tigers are now ....

13 Books, films and music

1 Talking about books and films

Complete the sentences about books with the words in the box.

chapters	in translation	rhyme
classics	one-dimensional	sitting
developed	page-turner	
heavy-going	relate	

1. You can tell it was written by a man! All the female characters were just so ....! I couldn't .... to them at all! He could've .... them far more.

2. It's one of the .... of Russian literature, although I've only read it ....

3. I read the whole thing from cover to cover in one .... It's a real ....

4. To be honest, I found it pretty .... I struggled through the first two .... and then gave up!

5. You call this poetry? It doesn't even .... !

Now complete these sentences about films with the words in the box.

convoluted	hyped-up	scene
cross	let-down	soppy
genre	moving	
gory	preposterous	

6. My girlfriend found it quite .... – she was in tears by the end – but I just thought it was .... , sentimental rubbish!

7. It's a horror film, but it's not that .... It works on more of a psychological level. There's this one .... where this woman emerges from a TV screen that scared me to death!

8. It's a film that defies .... , but at a push, I guess I'd describe it as a .... between an art-house film and soft porn!

9. It'd been so .... by everyone that I found it a bit disappointing, to be honest – a bit of a ....

10. I think at best you could say the plot was a bit .... – and at worst it was just totally .... ! I didn't believe any of it myself!

2 Talking about music

Complete the sentences with these words.

catchy	original	sampled
cover	rapped	solos
mainstream	remix	underground

1. He's a bit .... for my tastes. Even my mum likes him. I prefer more unusual .... stuff.

2. It's so .... I can't get it out of my head.

3. Her new single is a .... of an old 70s song. I have to say, I prefer the .... version.

4. It flopped when it first came out, but then they did a .... with a faster beat and it was a hit.

5. They've .... the drum loop from an old jazz record and then they .... in Japanese on top of it.

6. It's a killer track. It's got one of my favourite guitar .... of all time and a genius chorus.

3 *Won't*

Complete the sentences with these words.

admit	hurt	repeat	tell
get into	let go	say	
happen	let it lie	speak	

1. Go on. Stay. One more drink won't ....

2. You can tell me! I won't .... a word to anyone.

3. Her son's 21 now, but she just won't .... !

4. Ask her! She won't .... ME what happened!

5. I'm really sorry. It won't .... again.

6. I like the fact he won't .... to the press.

7. I know it was my fault, but he keeps going on about it. He just won't ....

8. He knows he messed up. He just won't .... it.

9. He was so rude! I won't .... what he called me!

10. The chances are I won't .... Cambridge, but it's got to be worth a try.

Which sentences are:

a. talking about things people refuse to do?

b. making predictions about the future?

c. making promises?

4 Unreal conditionals

Complete the conditionals with the correct form of *would* and the verb in brackets in the correct tense.

1. A: Did you go and see that film in the end?
   B: No. I .... if I ....
   (have to work)

2. A: You should've complained.
   B: I .... if it .... a more expensive kind of restaurant. (be)

3. A: Can you lend me some money?
   B: Sorry, I .... if I .... totally skint. (be)

4. A: Did you finish the work I asked you to do?
   B: I .... if the phone .... ringing! (keep)

5. A: Why don't you come out with us?
   B: I .... if I .... tonight. (work)

6. A: Do you go out much?
   B: Yeah, quite a bit, but I .... even more if I .... the money! (go out, have)

5 Reflexive verbs

Complete the sentences with the correct form of the verbs in the box and a reflexive pronoun – *myself*, *yourself*, etc.

beat up	excuse	pride	throw
do	hurt	shoot	top

1. Make sure you wear proper trainers for the run. You .... an injury if you don't.

2. I think the government .... in the foot with this latest decision. I can see it coming back to haunt them later on.

3. My date was so dull that I ended up .... and making an early exit!

4. The company always .... on offering excellent service and great value for money.

5. It's a pretty grim ending. The two main characters end up .... They .... off a cliff and drown!

6. There was nothing you could've done about it, so there's no point .... about it.

7. Boycott the supermarket if you like, but to be honest, you'll only be .... if you do. It won't make any difference to them!

6 Word building: people

Complete the collocations with the name of the person connected with the words on the left.

1. play the drums   a renowned ....
2. play sax   a .... in a jazz band
3. immigration has risen   an illegal ....
4. do heavy labour   a building ....
5. work in academia   a leading ....
6. traffic drugs   a gang of people -.....................
7. crack down on crime   a dangerous ....
8. it's rank hypocrisy   a total ....
9. resort to surgery   a top heart ....

7 Making arrangements

Complete the dialogue with ONE word in each space.

A: So what're you up (1) … tonight?

B: Well, I'm supposed to be (2) … out with some people (3) … work. They're going to some techno club, but I'm not really in the (4) … , to be honest. I'm looking for an excuse to get (5) … of it. What've you got on then?

A: Well, I was (6) … with the idea of going to the theatre. There's this play on called *Cyprus*, which I read a review (7) … – it sounds pretty good. I don't suppose you (8) … going?

B: Maybe. What's it about?

A: The secret service and the (9) … it's corrupted by politicians.

B: It sounds a bit heavy (10) … my liking.

A: Apparently, it (11) … have its funny moments and it's supposed to be very gripping. You sure I can't persuade you?

B: Maybe. I'm not usually (12) … that kind of thing, but it might make a change. Where's it (13) … ?

A: The Whitehall Theatre, but I could give you a (14) … , if you like. I'm driving there.

B: Oh, go on then. You've twisted my (15) … . What time?

A: Will you be back from work by six?

B: It's pushing it a bit. Can't we (16) … it later?

A: We could. But I haven't got the tickets, so I wanted to get there a bit earlier to be on the (17) … side.

B: Yeah. OK. Listen, it's fine. I'll just have to make sure I leave on the (18) … of 5.30.

8 | Relative clauses and prepositions

In English – especially spoken English – we prefer to keep prepositions with the verb or noun they go with rather than before the relative noun. For example:

There's a play on called *Cyprus*, <u>which I read a review of</u>.

NOT

~~There's a play on called *Cyprus* of which I read a review.~~

Add the correct missing preposition(s) to the sentences. The first one has been done for you.

1. Who's the person I need to speak *to* about tickets?

2. What was the name of that restaurant you went with your mum and dad the other day?

3. You know that band I was telling you the other day? They're playing at the Astoria, if you fancy going.

4. I still haven't heard about the film course I applied.

5. Do you know Jez? He plays in the basketball team I play on Sundays.

6. We went to a karaoke bar. It's not the first thing I'd think for a night out, but it was great fun.

7. Could you give me the full source of the article by Sue Sherrin you referred in your lecture?

8. I hope it's better than the last film he was, which I can't remember the name now. It was appalling.

9. We went bowling last night, which I'm absolutely useless by the way, and we had a great time. I went with the people I study Spanish.

9 | Listings

Cross out the ONE word or expression in italics which does NOT go with the words that follow.

1. *Ambitious / Challenging / Thorny* re-working of the classic Chekhov play, featuring *a seasoned / a long-running / an experienced* cast.

2. New play *loosely / fairly / closely* based on the *hard / harrowing / moving* true story of one soldier's capture and torture during the Second World War.

3. *Re-release / Re-make / Cover* of Billy Wilder's 1940s film noir classic, *Double Indemnity*.

4. Danny Theakston, one of the UK's *premier / premium / top* DJ's is behind the decks at Soup, the recently *revamped / renewed / renovated* venue in Dockside.

5. *A veteran / A quirky / An off-the-wall* comedy starring the *promising / up-and-coming / futuristic* young actor Vince Baldwin.

10 | Keywords for writing: sentence starter adverbs

We can use adverbs at the beginning of sentences to comment on the whole sentence.

Surprisingly, there has been a great deal of concern about the increases in interest rates over the last few months. *Unfortunately*, these increases were unavoidable.

Choose the most appropriate adverbs in these sentences.

1. *Admittedly / Regrettably*, we are unable to offer you a position at this time.

2. *Basically / Simply*, the reason for the lack of confidence in the directors was their sheer incompetence.

3. *Understandably / Interestingly*, he worked as an undercover agent before becoming an MP.

4. *Hopefully / Admittedly*, the profits were lower than expected, but this was largely due to unforeseeable circumstances.

5. *Happily / Understandably*, in a cold spell gas prices will increase.

6. *Hopefully / Luckily*, your investment will double in ten years.

7. *Worryingly / Regrettably*, there is a lack of the kind of leadership that might turn the company around.

8. *Remarkably / Unsurprisingly*, the company survived, despite losing millions on the deal.

Complete these sentences with the adverbs in the box.

basically	regrettably	unsurprisingly
luckily	remarkably	worryingly

9. .... , we are unable to give you a refund.

10. .... , although she is now one of the top violinists in the world, she didn't take the instrument up until she was 12.

11. .... , there is evidence that people are becoming more promiscuous and less careful in guarding against STDs.

12. .... , there were no other cars involved in the incident.

13. .... , share prices fell dramatically following the news of financial trouble at one of the country's biggest banks.

14. .... , I didn't have any choice but to accept their offer, even though it was much lower than I would have wanted.

14 War and peace

1 Collocations

Match the verbs with the words they go with.

bring about	prop up	step up
drum up	pull out	

1. .... their campaign / security / the hunt
2. .... the regime / the currency
3. .... reforms / regime change / peace
4. .... business / some enthusiasm / support
5. .... the troops / of the tournament / of the deal

Now match these verbs with the words they go with.

distract	hack	twist
fuel	intervene	

6. .... in the conflict / in a dispute
7. .... into a computer system
8. .... what I said / my words / my arm
9. .... us from the real issues
10. .... tensions / the economic boom

2 Word building

Complete the collocations with the correct form of the given words.

1. **dictate**
   a military .... , a .... boss
2. **precise**
   .... bombing, eight o'clock ....
3. **intervene**
   military .... , the .... years
4. **grieve**
   air their .... , ... bodily harm
5. **liberate**
   hailed as .... , sexual ....
6. **invade**
   an .... of privacy, see us as ....
7. **provoke**
   a totally .... attack, an act of ....
8. **fanatic**
   .... followers, religious ....

3 Death and dying

Complete the sentences with these words.

bled	choked	driven
broken heart	crushed	natural causes
childbirth	dragged	starved

1. He was stabbed in a fight and .... to death.
2. They carried out an autopsy on the body, but they concluded he'd died of ....
3. He got a bone stuck in his throat and .... to death.
4. His wife died in .... and he never got over it. He died of a .... a few years later.
5. I think she was literally .... to death by the press. They just wouldn't leave her alone.
6. The roof collapsed and he was .... to death.
7. A million people .... to death during the famine.
8. Her coat got caught in a car door and she was .... to her death.

Language note

If someone is *driven to death*, they're forced into a situation where they feel they have no choice but to kill themselves. You can also be *driven to kill*, *driven to drink*, *driven to distraction* or *driven to despair*.

4 Opposites

Complete the opposites with these words.

brainwashed	demented	impartial
break	get rid of	stick
censorship	gung-ho	

1. call a ceasefire   .... the ceasefire
2. government propaganda .... reporting
3. sceptical about the war .... about the war
4. a dignified statesman   a .... tyrant
5. our troops are loyal   their troops are ....
6. reporting guidelines   ....
7. prop up a regime   .... a regime
8. change your mind   .... to your guns

46

5 Key word: *war*

Complete the sentences with these nouns.

brink	crimes	reparations
casualties	hero	veterans

1. The victims of the mistaken bombing are just the latest .... of an increasingly bloody war.

2. Germany had to pay huge war .... after WWI.

3. Even though he was indicted for war .... , he was still hailed by some as a war ....

4. Many war .... suffered psychological problems years after returning from action.

5. In the past, Pakistan and India came to the .... of war over the disputed territory of Kashmir.

6 Reasons for war and conflict

Complete the sentences with these words.

annulled	dispute	install	overthrow
conducted	forcing	outlawed	

1. A left-wing group started a rebellion to .... the government and .... a Marxist regime.

2. The conflict grew out of racial tensions. The ruling majority .... ethnic cleansing, killing minorities or .... them out of the country.

3. The war was the result of a border .... where both countries laid claim to the territory.

4. The ruling government .... the elections and .... opposition parties, sparking a civil war.

7 A peace process

Put the sentences in the order the events happened. Number 4 is given.

a. As a result, the two sides broke off talks. ☐

b. Both sides declared a ceasefire and entered into talks. ☐

c. There was a breakthrough, leading to an agreement. ☐

d. The sides resumed negotiations. ☐

e. One side made tentative contact with their opponents. ☐

f. They signed a formal peace treaty. ☐

g. They conducted exploratory talks behind the scenes. ☐

h. The talks reached a deadlock. ☐ 4

8 Far from

We often show how things can have the opposite result to what's expected by using *far from + ing*.

Make complete sentences by matching the beginnings with the endings.

1. The government, far from crushing the revolt, ☐
2. Far from helping people out of poverty, ☐
3. Far from lifting people's mood, ☐
4. Research has found that, far from being unhealthy, ☐
5. Far from improving, ☐

a. their policies have widened the wealth gap.
b. created a breeding ground for opposition.
c. the situation has just deteriorated further.
d. a high fat diet can improve athletes' performance.
e. drugs and alcohol can exacerbate depression.

Complete the sentences with your own ideas.

• Far from helping the environment, ...
• Far from being upset at losing my job, ...
• War, far from ... , ...
• The government measures, far from ... , ...

9 *Battle* or *war*

Choose the correct word.

1. *War / Battle* had been looming for several months before it finally broke out.

2. The *warring / battling* parties have called a temporary truce.

3. The army is hoping the *war / battle* will be decisive in winning the *war / battle*.

4. The violence erupted after weeks of mounting tension and the police fought several running *wars / battles* with the rioters.

5. The country has been ravaged by *war / battle*, leaving it with almost no infrastructure.

6. The government's fighting a losing *war / battle* against drug trafficking.

7. The UN urged both sides to engage in dialogue in order to avert *war / battle*.

8. It's a constant *war / battle* trying to get my children to eat their vegetables.

9. The government has lost the *war / battle* of ideas and now it looks as if it'll lose the election.

10. I had to have a real *war / battle* with the airline to get compensation for the luggage they lost.

1 Sample report

Complete the report with the words in the box.

apart	gained	proportion	slightly
bar	graph	proposals	steeply
favour	little	rate	surprisingly

Castle View Road is an accident black spot and various (1) ... have been put forward to make the road less dangerous. The (2) ... shows the number of accidents that have occurred here since 2000 and the (3) ... chart shows the results of a survey of the residents of Castle View Road regarding their preferred proposal. The results have been divided into the opinions of those aged over 40 and those between the ages of 21 and 40.

We can see very clearly from the graph that (4) ... from 2002 to 2003, the number of accidents has increased at an alarming (5) ... . The number has risen most (6) ... in the last two years and stands at an annual figure of 48.

We can see from the bar chart that in the 40-plus age range a considerable (7) ... – over 70 per cent – favour a reduction in the speed limit from 40 mph to 30 mph between Fair Hill and Castleton itself. Of the other options, road-straightening measures were the least popular, with only 3 per cent supporting this proposal. There was also very (8) ... support for the new road-narrowing alternative, although speed humps were (9) ... more popular.

In the 21–40 age range, not (10) ... , the reduction in the speed limit was not very popular, with only 15 per cent in favour. Road-narrowing and speed humps, as with the older age group, also (11) ... little support. The most popular measure by far, with a staggering 69 per cent in (12) ... was the road-straightening option. However, only a tiny 1 per cent wanted to see a pedestrian crossing.

There seems to be a clear link between the age of the householders and the traffic-calming measures they opted for in the survey. The statistics show quite clearly that speed is of more concern to the older residents, who believe that a lower speed limit will slow the traffic down sufficiently to cut the number of accidents. On the other hand, the younger respondents opted for a straightening of the road to reduce the dangers. This latter group seem more prepared to tolerate the disruption that road-straightening would cause.

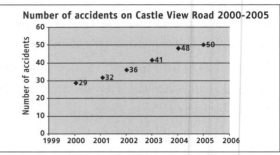

Number of accidents on Castle View Road 2000-2005

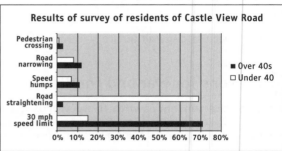

Results of survey of residents of Castle View Road

■ Over 40s
□ Under 40

2 Prepositions

Complete the sentences with the correct prepositions.

1. The local council has put ... a proposal.

2. The cafeteria has been divided ... two main areas.

3. Many people are ... favour of a total ban.

4. There is a clear link ... alcohol and liver disease.

5. We can see ... the results that few support the plan.

6. Students today tend to opt ... universities closer to home than they did in the past.

3 Collocations

Choose the correct collocation in each sentence.

1. The graph illustrates how the number of students in debt rose very *highly / steeply / largely* last year.

2. The statistics *obviously / clearly / certainly* show that many opposed the proposals.

3. The suggestion has *obtained / gained / made* little support in the area.

4. 58% of the respondents *agree / affirm / support* the proposal to create a car park.

5. The number of young people who smoke is increasing at an alarming *speed / rate / level*.

6. The proposed law is approved by a *shuddering / wide / staggering* 85% of the population to just 8% against.

15 Ceremonies, celebrations and culture

1 Weddings and funerals

Complete the sentences with these words.

aisle	civil	vows
best man	registry office	wedding list
bridesmaids	silver	

1. My brother got married last year. I was his
   .... and my little sister was one of the
   ....

2. Neither of them is that religious, so they just went
   for a .... ceremony in the local
   ....

3. While the bride and groom were exchanging their
   .... , I just got the giggles! I couldn't help
   myself!

4. I just got them a toaster from the ....
   they'd sent out with the invites.

5. We've been married 24 years now, so next year's
   our .... anniversary.

6. The bride looked so lovely as she was walking
   down the .... I got a bit tearful at that
   point, I have to say!

Now complete these sentences with these words.

buried	cremated	shrine
coffin	grave	tears
condolences	scattered	urn

7. My granddad was .... and his ashes were
   .... in a field near where he grew up.

8. When they lowered the .... into the
   ground, my mum just broke down in ....
   It was horrible!

9. I'm going to visit my gran's ....
   tomorrow. She's .... in a cemetery quite
   near here.

10. Can you pass on my .... to her family
    when you see them?

11. We keep the ashes in an .... It's part of
    a .... we have for all our ancestors.

2 *Needless to say*

Match the sentences with the follow-up comments.

1. I got the giggles in the middle of the ceremony. ☐
2. The doctor finally gave me the all-clear last week. ☐
3. My car got towed away last week. ☐
4. It'd been hyped up before its release. ☐
5. I finally crawled in at three in the morning! ☐
6. I thought I'd just sail through the exam. ☐
7. I caught the first episode by accident last month. ☐
8. It's bitterly cold in winter and unbearably hot in summer. ☐

a. Needless to say, it didn't live up to expectations.
b. Needless to say, though, I completely messed it up!
c. Needless to say, the other guests were less than impressed!
d. Needless to say, it's not exactly a tourist hotspot.
e. Needless to say, my dad completely hit the roof!
f. Needless to say, I'm now hooked on the series!
g. Needless to say, it cost a small fortune to get it released from the pound.
h. Needless to say, it came as a huge relief.

Can you translate *needless to say* into your language?

3 Tears and crying

Complete the sentences with these words.

cry	floods	tear
crying	sobbing	tears

1. It was so beautiful I just burst into ....

2. I felt so nervous on the morning of my wedding. I
   had a good .... , though, and felt better.

3. My son burst out .... when he found out
   Father Christmas isn't real.

4. I have to admit, the last scene of *Titanic* did bring a
   .... to my eye.

5. People were .... in the church when the
   coffin came in. They were in .... of tears.

4 Groups of people

We use some adjectives as nouns to talk about certain groups of people.

Complete the sentences with these nouns.

the dead	the living	the rich
the elderly	the needy	the unemployed
the homeless	the poor	

1. Did you see that that big banker they arrested for drink-driving got off with a fine? It's typical! There's one law for .... and another for .... !

2. I know you shouldn't speak ill of .... , but in this case, I'll make an exception! He was horrible!

3. I spent Christmas helping out in a hostel for .... in the centre of town.

4. Old people's homes are a real rarity in my country. Usually the extended family takes care of ....

5. I think the real issue facing the government is how to get .... back to work as quickly as possible.

6. I just think that those of us who are slightly better off have a moral duty to help ....

7. The big question, once .... have been rescued and the dead buried, will be how it happened.

Language note

We use *I for one* to emphasise our opinion, often when others disagree or haven't decided. For example: The case isn't finished, but *I for one* think he's guilty.

5 *Whoever, however, wherever, etc.*

Rewrite these sentences using words ending in -ever.

1. We don't have any kind of dress code at work.
   I can basically ....

2. I'm going to get this essay finished – even if it takes me all night! I'm going to get this essay finished ....

3. My boss sends me to all kinds of places. I don't have much choice in the matter. I basically have to go ....

4. I don't know who told you that, but they were wrong. .... misinformed you, I'm afraid.

5. I've tried phoning lots of times, but the line's been busy all day! .... , the line's been busy.

6. I'll pay for it, no matter how expensive it is.
   I'll pay for it, ... costs.

6 Different ceremonies

Complete each description with one of the groups of words, putting the words in the correct order.

awards + dignitaries + do
released + played + laid
washed down + attended + entertained
watching + symbolising + cheering

1. A procession of war veterans and victims .... wreaths at the memorial. A lone trumpeter .... and was followed by a two-minute silence, after which 20 doves were .... into the sky.

2. The launch of the company's new design was .... by 5,000 of their employees, who were .... by circus performers and singers. There were canapés with the best Iranian caviar .... with champagne.

3. The .... ceremony was a black-tie .... , held in a hotel, with local and national .... in attendance.

4. The ceremony dates back hundreds – possibly thousands – of years. A huge wooden phallus .... the fertility of the earth is carried into the village to .... from the .... crowds. It is then 'blessed' with rainwater.

Decide which ceremony is:

a. ancient   b. formal   c. lavish   d. solemn

7 *Considering*

Complete the sentences with expressions using *considering*. Use the words in brackets.

1. *Considering how little I paid for it* , my bike's lasted a long time. (little / paid)

2. I'm amazed I did a day's work, ... when I woke up. (ill / felt)

3. It's amazing how successful he's been, ... (young)

4. She was amazingly calm, ... (dangerous / situation)

5. They provide an amazing service, ... (few / resources)

6. The clients want us to finish the work by Friday, but .... I think that a bit unrealistic. (long / taken / so far)

7. We did well to only lose 2–1, ... because of injury. (many players / missing)

8 Prefixes

Match the prefixes with the words they go with.

anti	hyper	post	pro	sub
counter	over	pre	semi	under

1. .... inflation / active / tension / critical

2. .... life / European / democracy / war

3. .... indulge / grown / due / compensate

4. .... natal / grad / modern / script / war

5. .... tax / war / recorded / paid

6. .... depressant / clockwise / social

7. .... achieve / funded / estimate / nourished

8. .... attack / productive / act / balance

9. .... professional / skimmed / final / conscious

10. .... zero / text / human / consciously

Complete these sentences with the correct form of nine of the words above.

a. I really over......................... over Christmas. I must've put on six kilos.

b. I wish I'd never decided to do up the house myself. I under......................... how much work it would be.

c. My mobile's pre......................... , so I don't have to mess around getting top-ups all the time.

d. There is a big pro-......................... movement in the States, which opposes abortion.

e. That child is hyper......................... ! He never sits still.

f. Just bossing people around can be counter-......................... because it makes people resentful.

g. After having the baby, she suffered from post-......................... depression, so she was on anti-......................... for a while.

h. Maybe sub......................... I wanted him to win, which is why I didn't play as well as I could.

9 Key words for writing: contrast (1)

We use several different expressions to contrast different ideas or facts within a sentence.

Unlike people who lived a hundred years ago, our standard of living is very high. We have electrical gadgets to help us *whereas* they had to do everything by hand.

Complete the sentences with *unlike* or *whereas*.

1. The English enjoy a fried breakfast, ... the French, who prefer something lighter.

2. Margaret Thatcher liked confrontation .... the current PM tries to avoid it.

3. Men retire at 65 .... women retire at 60.

4. Whisky can be bad for your health, ... red wine, which is apparently quite good for the heart.

5. .... New York, London has a huge number of parks and green spaces.

Complete the sentences with these words.

compared	contrast	opposed
comparison	contrasted	

6. Many people believe that private schools and colleges offer a superior education .... to state schools.

7. House prices in the south of England have slowed down dramatically, as .... to those in the north, which are still rising rapidly.

8. In .... to some studies, we did not find a strong correlation between vitamin C supplements and viral prevention.

9. The government's upbeat predictions about growth .... sharply with analysts' views.

10. Growth in the final quarter was weak in .... to last year's performance.

Join these sentences with the words in brackets. Make any other necessary changes.

11. There is a lot of violence in films today. Thirty years ago, it was less common. (compared)

12. The English eat dinner early. The Spanish eat much later. (unlike)

13. A large number of children spend much of their free time on the computer. Ten years ago, they did sport. (opposed)

14. There are no restrictions on the days lorry drivers can drive in Britain. In France they can't drive on Sundays. (whereas)

16 Health and medicine

1 Health, illness and injury metaphors

Complete the sentences with the adjectives in the box.

bruised	fatal	infectious	sick
crippled	healthy	lame	unhealthy

1. You don't seriously expect me to believe that, do you? It's such a .... excuse!

2. His interest in computers verges on the .... !

3. I made the .... mistake of going on a date with my boss! What on earth was I thinking?

4. He was passed over for promotion, so his ego's a bit .... at the moment!

5. She's a great teacher. Her enthusiasm is highly ....

6. People who kill animals for fun must be .... in the head!

7. We made a very .... profit last year.

8. A lot of poor countries are .... by debt.

Now complete these sentences with the nouns in the box.

cancer	ills	scars	wounds
headache	pain	symptom	wounds

9. My ex wants to meet up and talk through our break-up, but I just don't see the point of reopening old ....

10. The whole country still bears the .... of the civil war.

11. The riots were just a .... of how alienated and angry many people feel.

12. Mike's not coming tonight. He didn't get that contract he was after, so he's at home, licking his .... !

13. You can't just blame all the .... of the world on the Prime Minister!

14. I hate going to the gym, but you know how it is – no .... , no gain!

15. Fear can eat away at you like a ....

16. The car has been a constant .... , to be honest. It's been one thing after another!

2 Word building

Complete the sentences with the correct form of the words in brackets.

1. So what did the doctor say? What was the .... ? (diagnose)

2. MS is basically an .... disease. (treat)

3. She was so worried about the flu that she went to the doctor's and got a .... against it. (vaccinate)

4. We use the coursebook in class and then there are some .... activities for us to do on the Web. (supplement)

5. The tube strike brought about an almost complete .... of the city. (paralyse)

6. I work with computers, so run quite a high risk of getting RSI – .... strain injury. (repeat)

7. The attack completely .... her. (traumatic)

8. We had a rat .... in the house last year. (infest)

3 Talking about time

Complete the sentences with the words in the box.

eleventh	halfway	last	run-up
golden	height	nick	wake

1. Football fever has gripped the nation in the .... to the forthcoming World Cup.

2. The 70s were a .... age for American films. So much good stuff came out back then.

3. They called off the strike at the .... minute.

4. They almost went bust a few years ago, but a new investor came in at the .... hour and saved their necks!

5. He stormed out .... through the meeting!

6. When she was at the .... of her fame, she must've been earning upwards of a million a month!

7. What struck me was how calm the city was in the .... of the attacks. It was like nothing much had really happened!

8. We got to the airport in the .... of time – five minutes later and we would've missed our plane!

4 Fighting fit

Complete the article with ONE word in each space.

Fighting fit

Belinda Lopez (1) ... from a rare hereditary disorder, which means her body doesn't break down certain fats, (2) ... her arteries to clog. This, in turn, can (3) ... to heart attacks. The condition can be controlled by maintaining a strict (4) ... which minimises fat intake. However, there is an inevitable deterioration with age. Her father suffered a (5) ... of heart attacks before having a triple by-pass (6) ... and in the future he may require a heart transplant.

Belinda and her family are campaigning to (7) ... awareness of the problem, which affects one in 10,000 people, and to increase funding for research. And it's the area of research where they have (8) ... with controversy. The scientists leading the research believe stem cell therapy is the (9) ... forward, but have met with (10) ... from people who see experiments using human embryos as not respecting the sanctity of (11) ... . They have argued that the research into a disease that is treatable, albeit through operations, is sending us further down a slippery (12) ... .

5 Disease and war

Complete the sentences with these words.

attack	defence	fighting	minefield
battle	fight off	lost	territory

1. Harriet Jones, the star of *Best Men*, has .... her long .... with cancer. She was 43.

2. I think we're entering dangerous .... when it comes to transplants with organs from animals.

3. Doctors performed an operation to remove the clot from the boy's brain, but he is still in a very critical condition and they say he's .... for his life.

4. The area of fertility treatment is a ....

5. The disease prevents production of antibodies, the body's primary .... against microorganisms, so the child can't .... infections.

6. The disease causes the immune system to form abnormal antibodies that .... the body's own organs rather than viruses.

6 I'll be doing / I'll have done

Complete the dialogues with the verbs in brackets in the future continuous or the future perfect.

1. A: What are you doing at Christmas?
   B: I imagine I .... to my parents', but I haven't actually discussed it with my wife yet. (go)

2. A: How's the job going?
   B: It's OK. I'm sticking with it for the moment, but I think by this time next year I .... enough of it, so I reckon I .... to move on next summer. (had, look)

3. A: Have you spoken to Phil? Do you think he .... that he needs to bring some form of ID to register?
   B: No. Maybe we should ring him now. I doubt he .... yet. You know what he's like. (remember, leave)

4. A: I'm really excited about this trip to Chile in December.
   B: I bet. I wish I could come with you, but I .... over my books revising for my exams while you two are sunning yourselves on the beach.
   A: Sorry, I didn't mean to rub it in. I .... of you and I'll have my fingers crossed for you. (slave, think)

5. A: Do you think you .... the designs by tomorrow?
   B: I doubt it. I thought you said you didn't need them till Tuesday.
   A: I know, it's just that I .... your office tomorrow on my way to another meeting and I thought I could pop in and pick them up.
   B: Oh right. No. I .... a rough draft of everything, but not the completed versions. I was going to courier them to you. (finish, pass, do)

Language note

If you *slave over* or *slave away at* something, you work very hard at it. For example:
I've *been slaving over* a hot stove all afternoon.
He's *been slaving away at* the project for months.

Writing: Reviews

1 | Sample review

Complete the review with the words in the box.

accomplished	manuscript	treated
array	merges	weight
concerned	scope	
justice	screen	

Bleak House, BBC 1, Thursday/Friday 8.30 pm

There have been decidedly mixed reactions to previous adaptations for television of Charles Dickens' *Bleak House*. Some critics insist that it is impossible to do (1) ... to a book of such complexity on the small (2) ... .

As far as I am (3) ... , any adaptation of one of the greatest English writers is worth seeing. In my opinion, the enormous (4) ... of Dickens' imagination shines through whatever mess directors may make of his works.

However, in this case, Andrew Davies, whose previous adaptations include *Pride and Prejudice*, has done a marvellous job. As always, the vast (5) ... of eccentric characters provide our most (6) ... actors with the vehicle for superb cameos. We are (7) ... to excellent performances from stars with such diverse backgrounds as *The X-Files* and stand-up comedy. Veteran actors Dennis Lawson and Charles Dance lend (8) ... to the high level of performance, and the brilliant Pauline Collins does a superb portrayal of the magical Miss Flite.

Performances apart, this interpretation of the Dickens classic is pacy and gripping. Returning to the manner in which the original (9) ... was presented to the public (in magazine instalments), the BBC has chosen to deliver it to us in short bursts of 30 minutes twice a week, rather like a soap opera. The characters scurry across our screens and scene (10) ... into scene without a second's break as the plots and subplots unravel. There is certainly no time for boredom to creep in.

Whilst the original novel has defeated many readers in the past, due to its density, this adaptation is – for me at least – highly compulsive viewing. I thoroughly recommend a visit to *Bleak House*.

2 | Collocations

Match these words to make collocations.

1. mixed   a. array
2. vast   b. reactions
3. diverse   c. viewing
4. stand-up   d. comedy
5. compulsive   e. recommend
6. thoroughly   f. backgrounds

Complete these sentences with the collocations.

7. Last night saw the emergence of a new talent in the field of ....

8. A host of performers from hugely .... come together in this wonderful production.

9. This new thriller series is proving to be ....

10. The film features a .... of stars.

11. I can .... this book.

12. The series has met with decidedly ....

3 | Adding information

Complete the sentences with a relative pronoun.

1. Andrew Davies, ... previous adaptations include *Pride and Prejudice*, has done a marvellous job.

2. Tom Cruise, ... previously worked with Spielberg in *Minority Report*, stars again in this thriller.

3. The film, ... has been beset by delays, is finally being released in June.

4. Kim Hills, ... gives a wonderful, albeit brief cameo performance, steals the show.

5. Critics of the film, of .... there are many, point to the miscasting of Ben Thor in the lead role.

6. The film, ... political overtones have caused controversy, has nevertheless been a smash hit.

4 | Practice

Write a review. Decide:

- how to briefly describe the plot of the film
- which facts about the director/actors you want to add
- what aspects of the production were good/bad

Grammar: Suggesting and recommending

1 Making suggestions

Complete the conversations with the words in brackets in the correct form.

1. A: I don't suppose you know a good vet, do you?

    B: No, sorry. .... a web search? (you / try / do)

    A: Yes, but there were literally hundreds!

2. A: Do you know where I can get something to eat?

    B: I guess you .... the café over the road. (try)

3. A: I really want to give up smoking, but I just can't.

    B: .... those nicotine patches yet? (you / try)

    A: No, I .... , actually. Maybe I .... them a try. (give)

4. A: Do you think I should take the Proficiency exam?

    B: If I .... you, I .... and improve my English a bit more. You .... taking it next year. (be, wait, try)

    A: Yeah, you're probably right.

5. A: What do you think I .... about it? (do)

    B: Well, if it .... me, I .... it time and wait and see what happens. (be, just give)

2 Reporting suggestions and advice

Complete these sentences with the correct forms of *suggest, suggestion, advice* or *advise*.

1. I did tentatively .... that last week!

2. They've .... everybody not to drink the tap water.

3. She gave me some sound .... about which exam to try.

4. I took my host family's .... and went to the doctor about it. He just .... me to take it easy and get some rest.

5. The doctor .... I avoid stress for a while!

6. Is it OK if I make a .... about the design?

7. Look, if I want your .... , I'll ask for it, OK!

8. He came up with some fairly ludicrous ....

3 Asking for and making recommendations

Complete the conversations with ONE word in each space.

1. A: I'm really into techno and house music.

    B: Oh really? Well, in that case, you .... check out this new club that's just opened up.

2. A: Maybe you .... to try that hairdresser's up the road. It's got quite a good reputation.

    B: Yeah, someone else told me they'd .... good things about it. Maybe I'll give it a ....

3. A: Hey, have you seen that film *A Brilliant Mind* yet?

    B: No, I haven't. What's it like? .... good?

    A: It's a .... ! You've .... to go and see it!

4. A: Have you been to the Tower of London yet?

    B: No, not yet. What's it .... ?

    A: It's great – well .... a visit.

5. A: I didn't think .... of *Ocean's Thirteen*. I'd give it a .... if I were you.

    B: Oh really? Thanks for the .... !

6. A: Have you been to Madame Tussaud's yet?

    B: No, not yet. Why? What's it like? Any good?

    A: Well, it's probably OK if you're .... that kind of thing, but it wasn't my cup of .... I wouldn't .... going there if I were you.

4 Talking about recommendations

Complete the sentences with these words.

| came up with | implement | strongly |
| highly | rejected | |

1. The boss just .... the recommendations out of hand!

2. The boss promised to .... the recommendations in full.

3. I'd .... recommend you get legal advice before signing.

4. The staff .... some very pertinent recommendations.

5. The hotel came .... recommended by friends of ours.

17 Humour

1 Jokes and laughter

Choose the correct word.

1. It was hilarious! We all *fell / burst* around laughing.

2. I nearly laughed my head *off / up*.

3. We *played / told* this great practical joke on Tom. We put all the clocks forward an hour, so he thought he was late!

4. It's good you can see the *funny / witty* side of it.

5. He's such a funny guy! He *breaks / cracks* me up.

6. The Irish are still the *butt / goal* of a lot of racist jokes in England.

7. She's got no sense of humour. She *takes / feels* everything so seriously.

8. He's very touchy. He can't *accept / take* a joke.

9. I like to *tease / joke* him about his pronunciation, but sometimes he gets really annoyed about it.

10. I was really upset about it, actually, but I tried to *smile / laugh* it off.

11. Go on then! Have a good laugh at my *expense / cost*.

12. I just couldn't keep a *serious / straight* face.

2 *Self-* adjectives (1)

Match the adjectives with the nouns they go with.

1. self-deprecating ☐   a. leader
2. self-inflicted ☐   b. instructions
3. self-appointed ☐   c. wounds
4. self-made ☐   d. smile
5. self-satisfied ☐   e. man
6. self-explanatory ☐   f. sense of humour

Now match these verbs with the nouns they go with.

7. self-catering ☐   g. group
8. self-help ☐   h. Internet addict
9. self-fulfilling ☐   i. politicians
10. self-confessed ☐   j. habits
11. self-serving ☐   k. holiday
12. self-destructive ☐   l. prophecy

3 *Self-* adjectives (2)

Complete the sentences with the words in the box.

self-centred	self-indulgent
self-conscious	self-pitying
self-disciplined	self-reliant
self-important	self-righteous

1. She's 81 now, but she's still very .... – she does everything for herself and always refuses our offers to help!

2. I couldn't work from home. I'm not .... enough. I'd never get any work done!

3. I know it's a bit .... of me, but I think I'll just have one last chocolate!

4. She's got this holier-than-thou attitude and is always moralising! She's so .... !

5. He's so full of himself! He talks about himself like he runs the whole company single-handedly. He's so ....

6. I weighed over 100 kilos and just used to feel really .... about my body.

7. Stop whinging! You're being so .... !

8. Why are you being so selfish and .... ? Why don't you think about what others want for a change?

4 Key word: *laugh*

Find 10 sentences with *laugh*. Mark the end of each sentence using /.

it'snolaughingmatterhetriedtolaughitoffbuticouldseehewas
reallyupsetaboutittheymustbelaughingallthewaytothebank
he'sbecomeacompletelaughingstockonlydiditforalaughitwas
alaughableofferinearlylaughedmyheadoffwehadthelastlaugh
you'llsoonbelaughingontheothersideofyourfaceyou'vegotto
laugh

Which of the sentences above have a similar meaning to the following?

a. I'm going to get my revenge on you.

b. They got a very good deal on this.

c. Everybody laughs at him and pities him now.

d. We may have lost the battle – but we won the war!

e. You shouldn't laugh about it. It's a serious business.

5 Ways of laughing

Complete the idioms with the words in the box.

cackle	giggles	laugh	stitches
chuckle	howl	roar	tears
giggle	hysterics	snigger	wet

If someone is a really funny person, you can say they're
(1) *a real* .... Perhaps they're always
cracking jokes or maybe they're just good at making
stories funny. If they make you laugh a lot, they (2) *have
you in* .... or (3) *have you in* ....
If you laughed a lot at one time, you can say you
(4) *had* .... *rolling down your face*. Some
people also say it was so funny they (5) *nearly*
.... *themselves* – though others think this
sounds a bit rude. Teenage girls often (6) ....
when the best-looking boy in the school goes past –
maybe because they're nervous or embarrassed! If adults
start laughing for some silly reason – in a childish kind of
way – they (7) *get the* .... Teenage boys
sometimes (8) .... *at* other people's
misfortunes or accidents. This is usually done in a cruel,
hurtful way. When you remember something funny that
happened or when you laugh softly, you
(9) .... *to yourself* about things. If someone
laughs like a witch, they (10) .... Old women
sometimes laugh like this! If you laugh very loudly and
for quite a long time, you (11) .... or
(12) .... *with laughter*.

6 Describing people's sense of humour

**Complete the sentences with the pairs of words
in the box.**

corny + sexist	mimic + impersonation
dry + deadpan	physical + slapstick
irreverent + go	punning + witty
mickey + sarcastic	satirical + critique

1. Have you ever read *1984*? It's very ....
   It's a kind of .... of autocratic
   governments.

2. He's got a very .... sense of humour. Half
   the time, I don't know if he's joking or not, he's so
   .... !

3. He takes the .... a lot and makes lots of
   .... little comments.

4. There's lots of word play and .... in her
   writing. She's very .... , but it can get a bit
   much too!

5. She's got a very .... sense of humour. She's
   not afraid to have a .... at those in power.

6. Their act relies very heavily on ....
   humour. There's lots of clowning around. It's all very
   ....

7. The guy's a dinosaur! His jokes are so ....
   – and he still does all those .... mother-in-
   law gags too.

8. He's an absolutely brilliant .... You should
   see his .... of the boss!

7 Should

**Complete the sentences with *should(n't)* and the
correct form of the verbs in the box.**

be	laugh	sit	think
bring	laugh	study	worry
go	see	take	

1. A: We .... really because we didn't know
   whether he'd hurt himself or not.

   B: I know, but it is funny when you see people
   slipping over – and on a banana skin as well!
   Classic!

2. A: Oh damn! I .... Pedro's book with me.
   He left it at my house the other day.

   B: Never mind. I can take it tomorrow. I
   .... him at college.

3. A: We .... and see that new Johnny Depp
   film. It's supposed to be hilarious.

   B: Yeah, I'd love to. I .... free on Thursday
   evening, unless something sudden comes up. I've
   got a meeting at four, but it .... that
   long, so we could go to the seven o'clock
   showing.

4. A: I'm really sorry. I .... , but you do look
   quite funny with your hair like that.

   B: Cheers! Well, you can stop now, OK!

5. A: I feel a bit guilty. I .... here watching
   TV. I .... !

   B: Chill out! It's good to take a break from work
   now and again. You .... so much.

6. A: He did apologise for laughing at me.

   B: I .... so too! He was horrible!

8 Euphemisms and political correctness

People often make up 'PC' terms as a joke. They describe people in a funny or ironic way.

Match the beginnings and endings to make complete sentences.

1. I'm not short, I'm just ☐
2. She's not fat, she's just ☐
3. I didn't lie, I was just ☐
4. I'm not getting old, I'm just becoming more ☐
5. I'm not tight, I'm just ☐
6. I wasn't wrong, I was just using ☐
7. He's not unemployed, he's just ☐
8. I wouldn't say he's clumsy. Let's just say he's ☐
9. It's not belching, it's just being ☐
10. I don't think of myself as bald, just ☐

a. alternative logic!
b. between jobs!
c. big-boned!
d. careful with my money!
e. comb-free!
f. economical with the truth!
g. experientially enhanced!
h. gastronomically expressive.
i. uniquely coordinated!
j. vertically challenged!

9 Doctor, doctor jokes

Match the first part of the doctor, doctor jokes with their punch lines.

1. Doctor, doctor, I tend to flush a lot. ☐
2. Doctor, doctor, my baby is the image of his father. ☐
3. Doctor, doctor, I keep seeing an insect spinning. ☐
4. Doctor, doctor, you have to help me out! ☐
5. Doctor, doctor, I feel like a pair of curtains. ☐
6. Doctor, doctor, I keep painting myself gold. ☐
7. Doctor, doctor, will this ointment clear up my spots? ☐
8. Doctor, doctor, I feel like a pack of cards. ☐

a. Well, pull yourself together then.
b. I never make rash promises!
c. Don't worry. It's just a gilt complex!
d. Never mind. Just so long as he's healthy!
e. I'll deal with you later.
f. Don't worry. It's just a chain reaction!
g. Certainly, which way did you come in?
h. Don't worry. It's just a bug that's going around!

10 Key words for writing: adding information

There are several ways of adding information and strengthening what has been mentioned in the previous sentence.

In addition to studying biology, he studied French and Latin.

He studied biology. *In addition to this,* he studied French and Latin.

Complete the sentences with the words in the box.

addition	also	furthermore
additional	further	not only

1. The proposed building will block the sun from shining on our property. .... , it will invade our privacy.

2. In .... to the students, there will be three members of staff on the coach.

3. .... does he train for three hours a day on the track, but he .... does weight training for an hour every evening.

4. An .... factor to consider is the number of guests invited.

5. A .... point to think about when buying a house is how near the schools are.

Did you notice what happens grammatically when we start a sentence with *Not only*?

Rewrite these sentences beginning *Not only*.

6. In addition to stealing money from the company, she lied about her qualifications.

7. He's been banned from driving for a year. Furthermore, he had to pay a £2,000 fine.

8. We should think carefully about the cost of the project. One further factor that should be considered is the environmental impact it will have.

9. The government is failing to reform the education system as well as failing to deal with the crisis in the health service.

10. There's a shortage of affordable housing in the area, on top of which the population is set to grow by 5 per cent.

11. He has consistently created great music. But on top of this, his whole lifestyle has been the envy of young men the whole world over.

12. It is in the EU's economic interest to act. More than that, however, it is also their moral duty.

18 Crime

1 Crimes

Match the words to make crimes which someone could be found guilty of.

1. grievous   ☐   a. assault
2. disorderly   ☐   b. and corruption
3. handling   ☐   c. bodily harm
4. indecent   ☐   d. the course of justice
5. reckless   ☐   e. evasion
6. obstructing   ☐   f. driving
7. tax   ☐   g. stolen goods
8. inciting   ☐   h. against humanity
9. armed   ☐   i. conduct
10. breaking   ☐   j. robbery
11. crimes   ☐   k. and entering
12. bribery   ☐   l. racial hatred

2 Passives

Complete the news reports with the verbs in brackets in the correct passive or active form.

Report 1

The actor Mervin Peterson (1) .... formally .... with failing to declare all his earnings. It (2) .... that the star (3) .... up to $10 million of undeclared income in various secret offshore accounts. (charge, claim, hide)

Report 2

Robbers (4) .... with £3 million in cash and bonds yesterday after hijacking a security van outside a branch of the Westminster Bank. Three men wearing balaclavas and carrying sawn-off shotguns (5) .... the driver, who (6) .... to hand over the keys. The driver, Ian Flitman, (7) .... for shock last night, but was otherwise uninjured. (escape, hold up, force, treat)

Report 3

Police (8) .... as sickening the wrecking of a local Indian restaurant by what they (9) .... mindless thugs. Chairs, windows and tables (10) .... and racist graffiti (11) .... on the walls during the attack, which occurred late last night. (describe, call, smash, spray)

3 Didn't I tell you what happened?

Complete the conversation with ONE word in each space.

A: So did you hear about any of that hooligan trouble while you were out in Portugal?

B: Yeah. We were actually caught up in the (1) .... of the whole thing.

A: You're joking!

B: No. It was pretty scary.

A: I (2) .... So where were you? What happened?

B: We were in a café in the main square (3) .... a pizza and there were quite a few English supporters around having a drink. I guess they'd had a few, but you know, it was pretty chilled, a bit of chanting, a bit of banter, but nothing obviously bad going (4) .... , so I don't know what really sparked the whole thing (5) .... I guess someone must've said something. Anyway, it just all kicked off in the bar opposite us. There were glasses and chairs (6) .... everywhere and then this other group suddenly came wading in and rampaging through the square, smashing the (7) .... place up.

A: That sounds terrifying. So what did you do? Were the kids with you?

B: Yeah! Poor little Harry was just in (8) .... of tears. The restaurant owners were fantastic. They took us inside the restaurant and led us into a back room until it all blew (9) .... I think it was a storeroom, but at (10) .... it was relatively safe. Anyway, we must've been stuck in there for about two hours. It was pretty grim.

> **Language note**
>
> If someone's *had a few* or *a few too many*, it means they have drunk a lot of alcohol – probably beer.
>
> *Banter* is playful conversation when people laugh and make fun of each other.
>
> If there's a fight or an argument and someone *wades in*, they suddenly join in, often without knowing what has gone before.

4 Prepositions

Complete the sentences with these prepositions.

by	of	of	to	with	without

1. She's been charged .... arson and insurance fraud.

2. The case has been referred .... the Crown Court, but at least that means you'll get trial .... jury.

3. He's long been suspected .... being involved in drug trafficking and other underworld activities.

4. He was convicted .... four counts of child abuse.

5. They want to bring in trial .... jury for some cases.

Now complete the sentences with these prepositions.

from	in	of	on	to	without

6. He was detained .... police custody for hours, and then released .... charge.

7. She was sentenced .... eight years in jail.

8. He's been released .... bail pending further enquiries.

9. My tutor's accused me .... plagiarising half the essay!

10. He was banned .... driving for a year.

5 Stages of a case

Put the sentences in the order the events happened. The first one has been done for you.

a. He got fifteen years. ☐

b. He was extradited. ☐

c. The police suspected him of involvement in a crime. ☐

d. He was held overnight for questioning. ☐

e. He was charged with the crime. ☐

f. He jumped bail. ☐

g. He went on trial. ☐

h. He made his first appearance in court. ☐

i. He was released on bail. ☐

j. He was arrested on suspicion of extortion. ☐

k. He fled the country. ☐

l. He was found guilty. ☐

6 Word building

Complete the sentences with the correct form of the words in brackets.

1. A tiny percentage of those given a .... sentence each year are aged 40 or over. (custody)

2. If he's found guilty, he's facing life .... (prison)

3. I think that sooner or later they'll be forced to .... cannabis. (crime)

4. Remember that woman who got life for killing her husband? Well, the High Court has overturned her .... (convict)

5. The article contained numerous .... (accurate)

6. He then proceeded to .... stab his victim in the neck and stomach. (repeat)

7. Mr James .... buried the bodies in his garden. (allege)

8. Shane Meadows is a .... underrated director. His last film was brilliant. (crime)

7 *Proceeded to*

If someone *proceeds* to do something, they do it after first doing something else. It often suggests that they did it in a thoughtless, uncaring way.

Complete the sentences with these pairs of words.

comes out + laugh	kicked in + slash
hack + alter	set up + transfer
hit + knocked over	slit + dismember

1. He .... his victim's throat and then proceeded to .... the body in his bathroom.

2. It was a .... and run. The guy .... this old lady and then proceeded to drive home like nothing had happened.

3. He .... several false bank accounts and then proceeded to .... a small fortune into them.

4. She .... the front door, smashed the TV and then proceeded to .... his entire wardrobe!

5. She just .... with some really odd comments sometimes and then proceeds to .... herself stupid about them.

6. He managed to .... into the school system and then proceeded to .... his grades!

Writing: Giving instructions and advice

1 Sample letter

Complete the letter with ONE word in each space.

Dear Kate,

It's really good to know you're covering for me while I'm away on the training course. Thanks so much. Knowing that you'll be teaching the kids is a real (1) .... off my mind. I'm sure you'll get on fine with them.

I thought I should leave you some notes on a couple of things that are planned for this week, and other advice that will hopefully see you (2) .... to next Friday relatively unscathed!

• Tuesday: The class is going to visit the Dinosaur Museum. Make (3) .... they take their notebooks and remind them on Monday to bring a (4) .... lunch and the entrance money.

• Thursday: I've promised them they can watch a Disney DVD as a special (5) .... It's in my locker. There are some worksheets to go with it. (6) .... the way, don't worry about marking them – I'll do it when I'm back.

• The photocopier is highly temperamental! A good kick will often suffice to (7) .... it working again!

• DON'T, (8) .... you do, use the coffee mug with 'The Snowman' on it – it's Dave's. He's incredibly possessive about it for (9) .... reason – just one of several things he's screwed up about! In fact, now I come to (10) .... of it, you're best avoiding Dave, full stop!

• The head is on the warpath about punctuality, so (11) .... warned! If you get to school even a minute past 8.15, she's liable to give you a real telling-off.

Seriously, (12) .... , you'll have a great week – the kids are wonderful. Don't let Mark and Jack sit together and you shouldn't have any disciplinary problems! Which reminds me, if you do have any problems, don't hesitate to mention them to the head. She's very supportive when it (13) .... to discipline. One last thing – could you leave notes on what you do, please?

See you in a fortnight's (14) ....

Best wishes,

Stef

Language note

We often add *full stop* to emphasise that this is our complete or final opinion. For example:

I know you say they are exceptional circumstances, but I just think stealing is wrong, *full stop.*

2 Warning and advice

Complete the sentences with these words.

be warned	I wouldn't recommend
could you possibly	make sure
don't worry about	remind
don't, whatever you do	you're best

1. Can you .... everyone the deadline is Friday?

2. There's a takeaway round the corner, but .... it. The food there's terrible.

3. .... cleaning the place before you leave. I'll do it myself once I'm back.

4. Before you turn in for the night, ... all the doors and windows are tightly locked.

5. .... , turn the pilot light off on the boiler. It's absolutely impossible to get started again.

6. .... , the guy upstairs does sometimes play his music really loudly!

7. If you want to do a big shop, ... trying the supermarket on the edge of town.

8. I'm really sorry to ask, but .... pop the books I've left on the table back to the library?

3 Changing tack

In more informal letters, we sometimes suddenly think of something we want to write. Find six words or expressions we use to do this. Then translate the expressions into your language.

nowIcometothinkofitwhileI'monthesubjectincidentallyby thewayjustbeforeIforgetwhichremindsme

4 Practice

You are going away for the weekend, and your friend is looking after your two children and your dog. Write some advice for her.

1 Health and fitness

Complete the texts with the words in the box.

check-up	moderation	six-pack
complaint	processed	symptoms
dominates	scratch	vice
fanatic	shape	
hypochondriac	sit-ups	

1. I'd describe myself as a pretty healthy kind of person. I try and steer clear of .... food as much as I can. I try and use fresh ingredients wherever possible and cook all my meals from .... I do drink, but only in .... and my only real .... is chocolate.

2. I think she's a bit of a .... She always thinks she's got the .... of some terrible disease and she's always going on about some imaginary .... or other. She must drive the doctor mad as she's in there for a .... every other day!

3. He's a bit of a fitness .... He's obsessed with having a .... , so he does about 300 .... a day! Don't get me wrong – he's in incredible .... , but staying that way just .... his whole life!

2 Staying in shape

Match the verbs with the words they collocate with.

1. work out ☐   a. a healthy diet
2. cut down on ☐   b. active
3. keep ☐   c. what I eat
4. take ☐   d. of junk food
5. stick to ☐   e. 50 lengths
6. eat ☐   f. rowing
7. snack ☐   g. vitamins and supplements
8. steer clear ☐   h. the amount I eat
9. watch ☐   i. on fruit and nuts
10. swim ☐   j. lots of greens
11. get ☐   k. at the gym four times a week
12. go ☐   l. plenty of sleep

3 Talking about how people are

Complete each conversation with one of the groups in the box, putting the words in the correct order.

agony + pulled + crutches	over + down + chucked
burn + knackered + dog	stiff + cramps + overdo
chest + round + down	tore + recover + operated
death + overdid + rough	wrapped + love + under

1. A: We must've been playing for about three hours and I got .... by the end. Honestly, I'm so .... this morning, I can hardly walk.

   B: You should be careful not to .... it.

2. A: I .... a hamstring when I was running and had to hobble two miles to get home.

   B: That must've been .... How long will you have to be on .... ?

3. A: I .... my cruciate ligament while I was away skiing in France and they .... on me out there.

   B: God, that's dreadful. So how long do they reckon it'll take you to .... ?

4. A: I'm .... I've been working like a .... recently.

   B: You need to be careful. It must be very easy to .... out in a pressurised job like yours.

5. A: I'm feeling really .... I .... it a bit last night.

   B: You do look a bit like .... warmed up!

6. A: She's feeling a bit .... the weather. I left her .... up in bed.

   B: Oh dear. Well, send her my .... I hope she gets better soon.

7. A: He's a bit .... in the dumps. His girlfriend .... him last week.

   B: What a shame. Still I'm sure he'll get .... it soon enough. Plenty more fish in the sea!

8. A: I think I'm coming .... with something. I can feel it in my .... and throat.

   B: I think there's some fluey virus going ....

4 | Football

Label the picture with the words in the box.

bar	laces	post
corner flag	net	shin pad
goal-line	penalty area	studs
keeper	penalty spot	touchline

1.	5.	9. ....
2.	6.	10. ....
3.	7.	11. ....
4.	8.	12. ....

5 | Talking about football

Complete the sentences with eight of the words from Exercise 4.

1. It was a nasty foul. He went into the tackle with his .... up.

2. We should've won, but their .... made a couple of incredible saves.

3. My .... were undone and I tripped over them just as I was about to shoot!

4. It's a free kick, because the keeper handled the ball outside the ....

5. I thought it was going in, but the keeper tipped it over the ....

6. They had a penalty, but they put it wide of the ....

7. It was a great chance. He should really have stuck it in the back of the ....

8. Their manager was on the .... , screaming the whole time!

6 | Adjectives

Match the adjectives with the nouns they go with.

civic	malign	salutary
cutthroat	mind-numbing	universal
foul	pathetic	unprecedented

1. .... attempt / joke / excuse

2. .... business / market / razor

3. .... delight / outrage / agreement

4. .... language / mood / smell

5. .... effect / work / boredom

6. .... lessons in life / warning / experience

7. .... influence / motives / effect

8. .... duty / pride / leaders

9. .... move / step / levels / growth

> **Language note**
>
> A *malign influence* is one that causes harm. If someone has been unfairly criticised, you can say they are *much maligned*.

7 | Sports idioms

Complete the idioms with the words in the box.

court	game	sailed	shot	towel
fish	horse	sea	sights	

1. We want to buy a house, but we might have to lower our .... and settle for a flat.

2. I'll give it my best .... , and if it doesn't work out, then I guess it wasn't meant to be.

3. I just about scraped through the exam, but my brother .... through with flying colours!

4. I've told you what I think. The ball's now in your .... It's up to you what to do about things.

5. I gave it my best shot, but after one awful grammar lesson, I decided to throw in the ....

6. The government needs to be very careful. Backing the wrong .... in a situation like this is a gamble that could well be paid for in blood!

7. When I found out they'd broken the contract behind our backs, I thought, 'Two can play that .... !'

8. I know she dumped you and it hurts, but there's plenty more .... in the ....

8 Playing cards

Complete the text with the words in the box.

ace	clubs	deck	lay
bluff	cut	hand	shuffles
chest	deal	jack	trumps

A pack or a (1) ... of playing cards has four suits: hearts, diamonds, spades and (2) ... . There are 13 cards in each suit – ace, king, queen and (3) ... plus the numbers two to ten. The (4) ... is usually worth most in a game. Before you start playing a game, someone (5) ... the cards. The person who does this is called the dealer. As the dealer, you might ask someone to (6) ... the pack before you (7) ... out the cards to all the players. The cards each person has is called their (8) ... , which can be good or bad. In some games, one suit is worth more than the other suits. This suit is then called (9) ... . We keep cards close to our (10) ... so other players can't see them, though in some games you (11) ... your cards on the table so other players can see them. In games such as poker you have to (12) ... – pretend to have better cards than you actually have.

9 Key word: *chance*

Make complete sentences by matching the beginnings and endings.

1. When he offered to take me hang-gliding, ☐
2. If England have got a full team out, free of injuries, ☐
3. Given the chance to live my life again, ☐
4. To be honest, I didn't think they'd have any tickets, ☐
5. It was a big thing quitting work for a job in Brazil, ☐
6. I think I blew my chances of going out with her, ☐
7. He missed the chance to play in the last Olympics, ☐
8. Getting a role in a film really was pure chance, ☐

a. I wouldn't change a thing.
b. but I just thought it was the chance of a lifetime.
c. I jumped at the chance.
d. I fancy their chances of winning the World Cup.
e. because he had a bad ankle injury.
f. but she really has grabbed it with both hands.
g. when I told her I smoked 30 cigarettes a day!
h. but I went on the off-chance that one might've been returned.

10 Key words for writing: contrast (2)

Match the sentence beginnings with the endings.

1. Even though it received excellent reviews, ☐
2. Despite descending ever further into debt, ☐
3. He invested his money in the shares, ☐
4. The event was deemed a huge success, ☐
5. In spite of the poor turnout, ☐

a. he continued to gamble.
b. even though everyone had advised him against it.
c. the event did actually manage to break even.
d. some organisational mistakes notwithstanding.
e. the film failed to win any of the major awards.

Now match these sentences with the follow-up comments.

6. He failed to get into Oxford University in 2005. ☐
7. The weather was atrocious. ☐
8. Parliament rejected the proposal. ☐
9. The gang covered their tracks very carefully. ☐

f. In spite of this, the government persisted with its agenda.
g. Nevertheless, the group continued the journey.
h. However, he reapplied in 2006 and secured a place.
i. Nonetheless, the police eventually caught them.

> ### Language note
>
> *Notwithstanding* is used in very formal writing to mean 'despite the thing or the fact just mentioned'.

Choose the correct words. There may be two possible answers in some sentences.

10. These theories are, so far, entirely without empirical support, *despite / notwithstanding / nevertheless* a few claims to the contrary.

11. Despite the massive rise in GDP over the last ten years, there *nevertheless / notwithstanding / nonetheless* remains a sizeable wealth gap.

12. The board have recommended we follow up on this suggestion, *despite / although / though* I personally feel we would do well to wait a few more days.

13. The package took three weeks to reach us, *despite / even though / nevertheless* it was sent first class.

14. *Despite / In spite of / Even though* the recent increase in profits, the road ahead still looks rocky.

1 Kinds of people

Match the kinds of people in the box to the statements about what they believe.

agnostic	fanatic	patriot
atheist	fatalist	perfectionist
cynic	nationalist	pessimist
disciplinarian	optimist	realist

1. Parents and schools are far too liberal. More corporal punishment wouldn't go amiss! ....

2. Most people just act out of greed. ....

3. It'll all be OK. Why wouldn't it be? ....

4. I wouldn't really say I'm religious, but at the same time, I would never say I don't believe in God. ....

5. I want my country to be completely independent and equal to every other country. ....

6. I got 98 per cent, which is OK, but it could've been better. ....

7. There's no point worrying about things. What will be, will be. It's all out of our control. ....

8. Oh well. Some you win, some you lose. That's the way the cookie crumbles, isn't it? ....

9. I think violence can be a legitimate means to an end. What's important is not the casualties, but the long-term goal. ....

10. I don't think there's a God. ....

11. There's no point bothering. We're going to lose. I've said so all along! ....

12. I love my country, and would fight to protect it. ....

Language note

Nationalist groups, *movements* or *leaders* aim to achieve political independence for an area or a group. However, far-right parties are also sometimes called *nationalist parties*. If a person is overly proud of their country, they might be called *a nationalist* or *nationalistic*. Both words have a negative connotation. Being *a patriot* or being *patriotic* generally has a less negative connotation.

2 Expressions with *and*

Match the verbs that commonly go together.

1. pick and	☐	a. change
2. mix and	☐	b. forget
3. chop and	☐	c. choose
4. rant and	☐	d. take
5. forgive and	☐	e. scream
6. give and	☐	f. rave
7. wait and	☐	g. match
8. kick and	☐	h. see

Now complete these sentences with the correct form of the pairs of verbs above.

9. I wouldn't trust that timetable. They keep .... it. It's different from week to week.

10. My boyfriend really wasn't keen to go out for dinner with my folks! He had to be dragged there ....

11. I was so annoyed about it I basically .... till I was blue in the face! All to no avail, though, of course!

12. Oh well, what's done is done. It's all water under the bridge now, isn't it? Let's just .... , shall we?

13. In any relationship, you need to learn to .... a bit. Compromise is crucial, isn't it?

14. I'm not really sure what I'll do after the course finishes. I'll just have to ....

15. There are four core modules and then you can .... from about 40 other options.

16. She's got great dress sense. She's really good at .... different styles – you know, vintage and designer.

3 Religious people and places (1)

Put the words in the box into the correct group.

chapel	mosque	synagogue
convent	priest	temple
dog collar	rabbi	turban
imam	rosary beads	vicar
incense burner	shrine	
minister	skull cap	

Places	Clothes/Objects	People
....	....	....
....	....	....
....	....	....
....	....	....
....	....	....
....		

Language note

Minister is used for the person who leads Protestant church services – *a Methodist minister, a Baptist minister, an Anglican minister.* Anglican ministers are also called *vicars.* Catholics refer to their clergy as *priests.*

4 Religious people and places (2)

Complete the sentences with these words.

carvings	mass	spires
confession	mat	tiling
congregation	Mecca	worshippers
leaf	sermon	

1. It's a huge mosque. They have over 5,000 .... there on a Friday.

2. There wasn't a very big .... at the service last Sunday, which was a shame because the minister gave a very good ....

3. My friend Sean is a fairly strict Catholic. He goes to .... and .... every week.

4. My friend Salim's a fairly devout Muslim. He always prays five times a day. He has a little prayer .... he carries with him and a compass, so he can pray towards ....

5. We visited the Dome of the Rock mosque in Jerusalem. It's amazing. The Dome is covered in gold .... and the .... is so beautiful – it has these fantastic vibrant colours and patterns.

6. We visited Cologne Cathedral, which was fantastic. You don't realise how high the .... are on photos, and some of the stone and wood .... are just fantastic – really intricate.

5 Key words: *faith / belief*

In each sentence, decide which words commonly collocate with *faith* or *belief*. One, two or three of the words may be possible.

1. I think that for some people, natural disasters can *shake / move / undermine* their faith in God, but for me, the response people have to events like that actually *repeats / reaffirms / reinforces* my faith in God and humanity.

2. A lot of people seem to have *deaf / dumb / blind* faith in the government – it's unbelievable!

3. I took the job under the *wrong / mistaken / misunderstood* belief that it would be a step up, but I actually ended up doing the same as I had been doing before.

4. The recent discussions have *fostered / encouraged / strengthened* the belief that a final settlement can be found.

5. Even after she started going out with someone else, he *hung / grabbed / clung* onto the belief that she would come back to him.

6. The company took a bit of a *leap / hop / stride* of faith in employing him. He had no experience really, but it's paid off.

Language note

Collocations can be difficult! Sometimes words can be interchanged with almost no difference in meaning and are equally common. For example, *shake/undermine* your faith. Sometimes words can be interchanged, but one is far more common than the other. For example, in the sentence *Contrary to widespread/common/popular belief*, all three adjectives can be used. They have more or less the same meaning, but by far the most common in this expression is *popular*. Other collocations are completely fixed – like *blind faith*.

Dome of the Rock

Writing: Letters of request

1 Sample letter

Complete the letter with the words in the box.

appreciative	mutually	understand
aware	pleased	wondering
behalf	possible	
kind	question	

Dear Mr. Skinner,

I am an English language teacher at the Gates School of English in Chichester and I am writing to you on (1) … of my students. I (2) … that you are visiting Chichester during the week beginning 3 November and I was (3) … whether it might be at all (4) … for you to visit the school and give a short talk to the students.

The students are aged between 18 and 30 and come from a variety of countries. My current class is fascinated by the political system in the UK and have been working on a project about our electoral system. I know that they would be extremely (5) … of a visit by a Member of Parliament.

I am well (6) … that you must be extremely busy and that your schedule may already be completely full, but I truly believe that you would find such a visit most rewarding.

If you feel that you could make time to visit the school, would you be (7) … enough to ask your secretary to contact our academic administrator, Miss Markham, who would be (8) … to arrange a (9) … convenient time. However, if such a visit is out of the (10) … , perhaps you would be so kind as to send the students a letter, which they could then include in their project.

Thank you for taking the time to read this letter and I hope to hear from you in the near future.

Yours sincerely,

Kelly Gilbert

2 *Would*

We often use *would* to make a sentence sound more tentative. For example:

Further negotiation is needed before we agree a price.
Further negotiation *would be needed* before we agreed a price.

Put the words in brackets in order to make common tentative expressions with *would*.

1. ……………………………………… (to / be / all / it / would / possible / at) cross-link some of the items featured on the site?

2. ……………………………………… (you / as / kind / to / be / so / would) examine the document thoroughly?

3. ……………………………………… (could / would / I / grateful / possibly / you / most / be / if) help with any suggestions or hints.

4. ……………………………………… (it / would / you / I / could / greatly / appreciate / if) get back to me about this as soon as possible.

5. ……………………………………… (enough / be / wondering / if / I / was / you / to / would / kind) forward this e-mail to the appropriate member of your editorial staff.

6. ……………………………………… (afraid / to / be / able / I / not / I / would / am) meet the suggested deadline. Could it be moved back?

3 Useful expressions

Complete the sentences with ONE word.

1. Could you do me a ……………………… and e-mail me with any suggestions you have for the portfolio?

2. I was ……………………… if there was any ……………………… you could find the original letter for me?

3. You wouldn't ……………………… to know anything ……………………… the speaker we have booked for next Friday, ……………………… you?

4. I don't ……………………… you could possibly do me a huge favour and explain the situation to Mark, ……………………… you? I ……………………… be incredibly ……………………… !

Grammar: Past tenses referring to different times

1 Past or present (1)

Decide if the sentences refer to the past or to the present/future.

1. I was thinking of going for a walk in a bit. Do you fancy coming?

2. I did ask him if he would mind if I brought along a friend, but he said no.

3. I was going to go, but something came up.

4. It's time we left. We'll miss our flight otherwise.

5. Would you mind if I switched over? There's a good film on the other side.

6. I wish I was more able to help.

7. If you didn't want to do it, why didn't you say?

8. I didn't realise you smoked!

9. I'll tell you what – if I was in charge, things would be very different!

10. It's about time the police did something about all the prostitutes and drug dealers who hang around there.

11. I think it'd be better if I spoke to him now rather than later.

12. I'd rather you didn't smoke, if you wouldn't mind.

13. I'd rather have gone somewhere else, but I didn't have much choice.

14. I didn't know you did flamenco dancing.

Find sentences from the above that match the following grammar rules.

a. We use past forms to show that we think a present situation is impossible or very unlikely.

b. We use past forms after certain expressions such as *it's time* or *I'd rather* when we use a clause rather than an infinitive or base form of the verb. For example: *it's time to go, I'd rather not do it.*

c. We use past forms to be more polite – often because they show tentativeness and allow other speakers to say no.

d. We use past forms after sentence starters like *I didn't know* when we discover something new and surprising.

2 Past or present (2)

Complete the sentences with a past or present form of the words in brackets. You may have to use negatives.

1. A: Did you see the re-run of *At home with the Pipers* last night?

   B: No! I .... it was on. I love that programme. I .... why they didn't do another series.

   A: No idea. It'd be great if they .... , though. (realise, wonder, do)

2. A: I .... vaguely .... of applying for the job as head of department. Do you think it's worth it?

   B: You might have a chance if you .... a bit more experience, but I'd just forget it, if I .... you.

   A: Thanks for the support! Remind me to encourage you if you .... anything similar!

   B: Don't get all defensive! I'm just trying to be honest. If you .... me, it's about time they .... a bit of new blood at the top – it's just that they never do, do they? They always go for the same old faces. (think, have, be, do, ask, introduce)

3. A: Would you mind if I .... early today?

   B: I'd rather you .... , to be honest.

   A: Oh, come on! It's not as if I .... always .... home early. If it .... urgent, I wouldn't have asked.

   B: I know. It's just that we .... a massive backlog of work to clear and if we .... to grips with it, we're going to be inundated with complaints. (leave, do, go, be, have, get)

4. A: If you ask me, it's about time they .... pandering to public opinion and .... actually making some brave decisions – even if it .... being unpopular!

   B: Yeah, maybe, but it's easier said than done, isn't it? I mean, would you .... your job by doing something like that, if you .... in their position? (stop, start, mean, risk, be)

21 Travel and tourism

1 Accidents and near misses

Complete the sentences with these words.

clipped	dodge	skidding	windscreen
crashing	opened	straight	
cut	ran out	swerve	

1. He went .... through a red light.

2. He went .... into the back of us.

3. He just suddenly .... right in front of me.

4. I had to .... to avoid him.

5. A dog .... in front of me.

6. He .... my wing mirror as he went past.

7. She went straight through the .... !

8. We somehow managed to .... the oncoming traffic.

9. He .... his door on me just as I was passing.

10. We went .... off the road.

Language note

We use *go* and *come* with several verbs connected to movement. Your flatmates might *come barging into your room*. Your little sister might *come waltzing in* three hours after she said she'd be home. When you're playing football, someone could *come charging in* with a hard tackle. An angry mob or a gang of football hooligans might *go rampaging through the streets*.

2 Car collocations

Match the verbs with the words they go with.

1. honk   ☐   a. my windscreen
2. put on   ☐   b. his number
3. grip   ☐   c. my wing mirror
4. shatter   ☐   d. the brakes
5. dip   ☐   e. your seatbelt
6. glance in   ☐   f. the gas
7. slam on   ☐   g. your horn
8. put my foot on   ☐   h. the boot
9. open   ☐   i. the steering wheel
10. get   ☐   j. my headlights

3 Animal idioms

Choose the correct word.

1. Are you sure his house is this way? This is starting to feel like a wild *goose / duck* chase!

2. It used to be a really nice area, but it's gone to the *wolves / dogs* a bit in recent years.

3. A: How did you hear? It was a secret.

   B: Oh, a little *cat / bird* told me.

4. I'd been having problems there for a while, so when they told me I'd have to work weekends – well, that was the straw that broke the *camel's / donkey's* back.

5. A: Who told you about the planned redundancies?

   B: Trust me. I got it straight from the *parrot's / horse's* mouth. I had a drink with the boss yesterday and he told me then.

6. I haven't seen Michael in *dog's / donkey's* years.

7. What's up with you? You're not normally this quiet. *Dog / Cat* got your tongue, has it?

8. I know I should probably just let sleeping *bears / dogs* lie, but I just want him to explain why he fired me.

4 *Wouldn't*

Complete the sentences with these verbs.

accept	budge	heal	listen
believe	download	leave	

1. I swore blind I'd had nothing to do with it, but he just wouldn't .... me!

2. I tried to say sorry, but he wouldn't .... my apology!

3. He was so stubborn. Once he'd made up his mind about something, he wouldn't even .... to other points of view.

4. He kept hassling me. He just wouldn't .... me alone.

5. I kept clicking on the icon, but it wouldn't ....

6. The wound just wouldn't .... It was horrible! It ended up going completely septic.

7. I tried to move it, but it just wouldn't .... !

5 | Key word: *blind*

Find 10 expressions and collocations with *blind*. Mark the end of each expression using /. Translate them into your own language.

theblindleadingtheblindblindobedienceblindinglyobviousin
myblindspotswearsblindblinduswithscienceturnablindeye
toitdoitblindfoldblinddrunkinblindpanic

Complete these sentences with the expressions.

a. He .... he sent me the
   letter. But I'm telling you, I never received it.

b. I didn't see him overtaking me because he was
   ....

c. I think he could've explained things in a simpler way.
   He was just trying to ....

d. I shouldn't really have pressed the alarm. I just did it
   ....

e. Our boss doesn't know what he's doing and neither
   do we. It's just ....

f. When he explained his plan, it just seemed so
   .... I couldn't understand
   why we hadn't done it before.

g. I'm so used to driving along this route I could
   probably ....

h. He turned up .... It was
   awful. We had to ask him to leave.

i. I think the soldiers should've gone against their
   general's command to shoot civilians instead of
   following orders in ....

j. People constantly exceed the speed limit, but the
   authorities just ....

6 | Word building: *out of*

Complete the sentences with the noun form of the adjective in brackets.

1. He said it out of pure .... (ignorant)

2. They smashed up the place out of sheer
   .... (bored)

3. He was shouting out of .... (frustrated)

4. I took the job out of .... (desperate)

5. He paid for it out of .... for my help.
   (grateful)

6. Can I ask you something just out of .... ?
   (curious)

7. She lied out of some weird sense of ....
   to him. (loyal)

7 | Road signs

Look at the signs. Match the signs with the sentences.

1. I can't believe I got a ticket. I didn't think I was
   exceeding the speed limit. I thought it was 70
   on roads like that. ☐

2. Look, that's probably the turning we want
   coming up. ☐

3. All these hairpin bends are making me feel
   a bit sick. ☐

4. Hey, you do realise you weren't supposed to
   overtake there. ☐

5. You do realise it was his right of way – which
   might have something to do with why he made
   that gesture at you! ☐

6. They were drilling in the road all morning. I
   think they were replacing a burst water main
   or something. ☐

7. You'd better slow down. There's a sharp bend
   ahead just before you come into the village. ☐

8. Oh no! You can't turn right here. We're going
   to have to go the long way round. ☐

9. Is there no other way? I don't think the car
   will make it up the hill. ☐

10. They should do something about this road –
    it's so full of bumps and potholes. ☐

Cover the sentences above and complete the collocations.

a. .... the .... limit

b. the turning's ....

c. a .... bend

d. it's .... way

e. replace a .... water ....

f. go .... way ....

8 Travel and tourism

Complete the postcard and e-mail with the words in the box. Use the correct form of the verbs.

accompany	hit	pick up	track
fund	jet	raft	trek
hang out	let	settle in	venture
highlight	lifetime	tomorrow	wish

Dear Kwarme,

We've been here in Malta for a week now. It's been fantastic. We haven't (1) ... far from the swimming pool or beach during the day, although there are supposed to be some great sights inland. To be honest, we don't feel like doing much after (2) ... the town at night. Honestly, people party like there's no (3) ... here and it's been great to come and (4) ... our hair down after the stressful days in the office. (5) ... you were here.

Love, Shaz

Millie,

Just an e-mail to let you know how things are going on our round-the-world trip. We've been in Thailand for the last few weeks. Last week we went (6) ... for five days in the remote valleys north of Chiang Mai. It was really off the beaten (7) ... , which made a change to the more touristy places we'd been staying in. There were ten of us (8) ... by a local guide and we stayed in stilt houses in two tribal villages. The tribal people were amazing – really warm and welcoming. As well as walking through the mountains, we went (9) ... down rivers, which was kind of scary for someone who swims as badly as I do, but also really exhilarating. However, I think the (10) ... must have been riding an elephant for half a day. Just unforgettable – the trip of a (11) ... . Mind you, it's still not finished. We're (12) ... off to Australia tomorrow, where I'm hoping to find a temporary job to (13) ... the next stage of our travels. If I don't, I might have to hitchhike home! It should be OK, though. We've been (14) ... with some Aussie guys here in Phuket and they've given us a few names of places where we should be able to (15) ... some work. Anyway, I'll e-mail you again in a couple of weeks once I've (16) ... .

Love, Romy

9 Key words for writing: cause and effect

We use a variety of different verbs to indicate cause and effect. Always try to notice the prepositions that follow them.

Last week's cold weather *was caused by* a ridge of low pressure coming in from the Arctic.

Complete the sentences with these words.

brought	factor	influenced	rise	stems
down	hand	led	role	triggered

1. A huge .... in the clothes retailer's success has been its ability to adapt to new trends and customer demands.

2. The PM's refusal to come clean about his role in the scandal .... to his political downfall.

3. The leaked documents have given .... to rumours about a tax increase.

4. The rumours of tax increases in the forthcoming budget .... a run on the stock market.

5. Insufficient controls on industrial waste have played a significant .... in global warming.

6. The bad results this year are .... to a lack of commitment from the players.

7. His policies are strongly .... by his upbringing and a firm belief in justice for all.

8. The current political uncertainty has been .... about by the vote of no confidence, which the government only narrowly won.

9. A lot of racism simply .... from ignorance of other cultures.

10. A number of different research teams have had a .... in the breakthrough in cloning technology.

Complete these sentences with the correct preposition.

11. The rivalry between the two countries stems .... a deep-seated hatred.

12. The disappearance of many animal species is mainly due .... man's greed.

13. Peace in the area was brought .... by long discussions.

14. Most cases of skin cancer are attributable .... too much exposure to the sun.

15. The staging of the jazz festival was a huge factor .... the increase in tourism last year.

1 | Describing people at different ages

Complete the sentences with the words in the box.

cheeky	out of control	snigger
crawl	over-protective	supportive
earnest	puerile	sweet
encouraging	rebellious	teething

1. Oh, bless! She looks so .... in this picture!

2. My dad's always .... us to stretch ourselves and try new things.

3. He's five months old now and has just started .... He's been drooling and sucking and chewing anything that comes near his mouth!

4. He's got this stupid 14-year-old's sense of humour! It's so .... ! I find it quite infuriating, to be honest.

5. I'm worried that he's getting .... He's got in with a bad crowd and had a few scrapes with the police. And whenever I try and tell him anything, all he does is .... at me behind my back!

6. He can be a bit of a handful on occasion. He's very .... sometimes – answering back all the time.

7. He's 16 now, and is going through a bit of a .... phase. He's dyed his hair and got a piercing!

8. She's nine months old now and has just started to .... , so I've been busy baby-proofing the house.

9. My folks have always been very .... of me – even when I got pregnant and dropped out of uni.

10. To be honest, I think you're being a bit .... I mean, he's 15 now, you know! I think you smother him a bit.

11. He's a very serious, ... kind of 18-year old!

2 | *Will* for talking about habits

We can use *will* and *won't* to talk about habits and typical behaviour.

Complete the sentences using the words in brackets. The first one has been done for you.

1. My son's only just started eating solid food, so *he'll sometimes gag or even throw up if the pieces of food are too big.* (he / sometimes gag / even throw up / pieces of food / too big)

2. My granddad and his friends .... (hours / reminisce / good old days)

3. He's so macho! Even when it's freezing cold, he .... (walk around / wear / T-shirt)

4. My brother's a complete slob. Most nights, he .... (pig out / McDonald's / wrappers lying around)

5. I'm worried he's got ADD. He .... ! (sometimes tell me his brain / not stop / round and round)

6. What we .... (usually / Xmas / a big family get-together)

7. My daughter's so funny. Sometimes what she .... ! (do / a whole jigsaw puzzle – upside down)

8. She's still pretty sprightly, but she .... (not usually / walk / more / few / hundred metres)

9. He's a smart dog. He .... (not normally do / I tell him / give / little snack / reward)

Language note

If someone is moaning to us and we want to tell them that we think something they typically do is stupid and that they bring problems upon themselves as a result of this, we can use *Well, if you will* ... . We stress *will* when we say it.

A: I think I'm coming down with a cold.

B: Well, if you WILL go out in this weather half-naked, what do you expect?

3 The pensions crisis

Complete the article with ONE word in each gap.

The pensions crisis

Various solutions have been put (1) ... to solve the so-called pensions crisis. Perhaps most controversial of all is the plan to raise the retirement age to 67 or (2) ... 69. Many feel that this is tantamount to abolishing retirement altogether – people will have to work (3) ... into the grave. Another approach is to compel citizens to make bigger (4) ... into their pension funds – often in private rather than state-run schemes – while a third is to cut the benefits pensioners will receive. Some parties have suggested that all three solutions should be adopted at (5) ... and the same time!

However, arguments that we are (6) ... a crisis in pensions and that we are all doomed to live in poverty in old age have been greatly exaggerated, (7) ... to some academics. While the ratio of under-65s (8) ... over 65s has been decreasing, some economists argue this is the wrong calculation. What (9) ... more is the relation between those in work and those in retirement, and that in these (10) ... the problem is much less severe than it may at (11) ... appear. In addition, they point to the (12) ... that as the economy grows through better productivity, then fewer people can sustain a bigger number of pensioners at a similar (13) ... of wealth. Finally, they argue that the statistics which focus (14) ... a falling birth rate also fail to take (15) ... of new immigrants, who will be almost (16) ... under the age of 65. Based on this analysis, (17) ... is required is merely good economic management by the government and the maintenance or slight increase of the (18) ... levels of saving.

Language note

If an action, plan or statement *is tantamount to* something, it has the same bad qualities as that other thing. For example:
'Victory attained by violence *is tantamount to* a defeat, for it is momentary.' (Mahatma Gandhi)

We can emphasise that something is the same thing or happens at the same time by using *one and the same*. For example:
It has been suggested that the writers Shakespeare and Bacon are *one and the same* person.

If someone or something *is doomed to* something, the future will end badly. For example:
The whole scheme *is doomed to* failure.

4 Verb collocations

Match the verbs from the text on page 129 of the Coursebook with the words they collocate with.

1.	bide	☐	a.	within spitting distance
2.	accrue	☐	b.	me down the river
3.	go	☐	c.	the rewards
4.	live	☐	d.	my time
5.	sell	☐	e.	about the good old days
6.	make	☐	f.	on the scrapheap
7.	be thrown	☐	g.	interest
8.	reap	☐	h.	in his ways
9.	be stuck	☐	i.	out of the window
10.	reminisce	☐	j.	my blood boil

5 Expressions with *no*

Write complete sentences with *no* expressions using the ideas in *italics*. The first one has been done for you.

1. *I / absolutely / desire / ever / children.* I just don't like them! *I have absolutely no desire to ever have children.*
2. *need / heat / milk* – the baby will drink it as it is.
3. *point / try / talk / them.* They won't listen.
4. *good / cry.* It's broken now. It won't help mend it!
5. The market's in a mess and *sign / things / improve.*
6. *really / excuse / behave / that way* – screaming and shouting like that!
7. *they / left / choice / sack him* after they found out how much money he'd lost.
8. They've just spent £350 on a buggy for their kid – *wonder / debt!*

6 Baby things

Label the pictures with the words in the box.

beaker	buggy	dummy	pram
bib	cot	playpen	rattle

1 .... 2 .... 3 .... 4 ....

5 .... 6 .... 7 .... 8 ....

Writing: Reports

1 Sample report

Complete the report with these words.

attitude	consisted	introduce	range
commented	findings	overall	regarding
consider	general	ran	

Report on College Cafeteria

This report is based on the (1) ... of a survey carried out over a four-week period during which all customers of the College Cafeteria were questioned. The survey (2) ... of questions relating to décor, comfort, quality and (3) ... of food and drink on sale, service and opening times. (4) ... , the results were not favourable. Several concerns were raised and these are outlined below.

Décor and comfort

In (5) ... , the cafeteria was praised for its cleanliness in the seating area. It was pointed out that tables seating larger numbers would be preferable as students enjoy sitting with classmates and often have to push tables together to accommodate larger groups. Students were largely happy with the décor, although some (6) ... on the cold atmosphere created by the cream walls, plastic tables and chairs, and blue-tiled floor.

Food and drink

(7) ... the items sold in the cafeteria, it was generally felt that the range of hot meals was limited and the quality sometimes questionable. A large number of students indicated that there were not sufficient healthy-eating options. Most meals consisted of pasta with chips, and few fresh vegetables or fruit. It was also thought that prices were inflated and the cheaper meals (8) ... out early.

Service

Another important point that came out of the survey was the (9) ... of the cafeteria staff. The serving ladies do not seem to have a good rapport with the students.

Recommendations

It is clear that certain points need to be addressed. It is extremely important to (10) ... more healthy options and to reduce prices. It is also essential to encourage a better rapport between students and staff. If the situation remains unchanged, the college should (11) ... employing another company to take over the running of the cafeteria.

2 Passives

Passives are common in reports. Complete these sentences with the correct form of the verbs.

be based on	be made	be raised
be conducted	be outlined	be rated
be implemented	be questioned	be singled out

1. This report .... an opinion poll which .... over the week beginning 29 July.

2. A representative sample of the electorate .... about the government's performance in a number of areas.

3. Several concerns over the level of service .... and these .... below.

4. The staff in general .... highly for the service they provide. The receptionists .... for particular praise.

5. A number of recommendations .... following customer feedback last year, but few, if any seem ....

3 Reporting

Reorder the letters in bold to make reporting verbs / expressions.

1. Several people **dtiicnaed** their preferences.
2. Several people **ptoiedn tou** errors in the brochure.
3. Respondents **ecmotdenm no** the lack of support.
4. A number **iovcde cnnorcse** over the food.
5. The customers **irpaeds** the attention to detail.
6. Some **seprexsde a dsriee** for kids' facilities.

4 Practice

Write a report on a hotel that you have been to or a company that you know. Decide:

- what evidence the report is based on
- what areas you are going to focus on
- what aspects of each area were good and bad
- if there are any direct quotes you want to include
- what recommendations you would make

23 Taboos and embarrassing situations

1 Awkward situations

Complete the sentences with ONE word in each space.

1. I don't know what you said, but it must've hit a raw .... because he went ballistic afterwards.

2. I was only messing around, but he made it very clear I was treading on thin .... !

3. I really put my .... in it, but how was I supposed to know that that idiot was her husband?

4. You shouldn't eat on the tube in Tokyo, because eating in public is a real .... – .... there.

5. No, you've got the wrong end of the .... It's not my current boss – I meant my OLD boss!

6. To be honest, the whole area of religion and politics is a bit of a .... subject with my parents. It's best just to .... clear of it altogether.

7. My son's got lots of food allergies, so eating out is a potential .... A forkful of the wrong food can be fatal!

8. He tried to cover up his mistake by saying it had just been a slip of the ....

2 Word building: verbs–nouns

Complete the sentences with the correct noun form of the verbs in the box.

blaspheme	marginalise	realise
infiltrate	perceive	view

1. The company still suffers from the .... that their cars are crude, cheap and comic!

2. The root of the problem was the fact that the architects never had a clear .... of what they wanted.

3. I think there's been a growing .... that the pensions system as it stands is unsustainable.

4. I work for an NGO, trying to combat the increasing .... of the poor in developing countries.

5. They should repeal the .... laws altogether.

6. The authorities fear large-scale .... of the security forces by militant groups.

3 Key word: *God*

Complete the sentences with these expressions.

God forbid	godsend
God knows	hope to God
God's gift to women	in God's name
god-awful	My God
godforsaken	play God
God-given	the fear of God

1. I feel dreadful! I had the most .... day at work. I need a drink!

2. I can't stand him! He really fancies himself! He struts around like he's ....

3. A: So how can she afford to stay here for another six months if she really is as poor as she says?

   B: .... ! I haven't the foggiest.

4. That money coming when it did was a .... I'd have been totally broke without it.

5. He just seems to think he's got a .... right to demand whatever he wants.

6. It was one of the most horrible, ... places I've ever been to in my whole life!

7. I just .... that we at least manage to get through to Round 2 of the World Cup.

8. .... ! Look! She's the fattest person I've ever seen! She's like a walking mountain.

9. The whole episode really did put .... into me. I've never been so scared in all my life.

10. A: Is that terrible girl Marcia in that class you're moving into?

    B: .... ! She'd better not be!

11. I'm totally opposed to euthanasia myself. I just don't think we have the right to ....

12. What .... do you think you're doing?

Language note

Some people think it's wrong to say the names *God*, *Christ* or *Jesus* in non-religious contexts. They may well see some of the expressions above as blasphemous. However, many people no longer view these expressions in this way and feel they are a normal part of everyday spoken English.

4 | *No sooner*

Rewrite the sentences so that they are more emphatic. Start each sentence with *No sooner*. The first sentence has been done for you.

1. As soon as I'd finished the sentence, an awkward silence fell.

   No sooner had I finished the sentence than an
   awkward silence fell.

2. The minute the question left my lips, I realised I'd really put my foot in it!

3. It was weird! Literally two seconds after I finished writing this letter to her, the phone rang and it was her!

4. Wigan equalised and then about 30 seconds later, Arsenal went up the other end and scored the winner!

5. It was scary. The lights went out just after the lift stopped and we were left in total darkness.

6. We were lucky! It started raining about five minutes after we finished putting the tent up!

7. The webcam started playing up the minute I plugged it in!

5 | Loan words

Complete the sentences with eight of the words in the box.

aficionado	ghetto	realpolitik
bravado	guerilla	solo
doppelganger	kitsch	stampede
embargo	macho	tirade
fiasco	mafia	zeitgeist

1. She was subjected to a .... of racist abuse.

2. The whole sorry project has been nothing short of a complete and utter .... !

3. Well, if it wasn't you I saw yesterday, then you must have a .... ! He looked exactly like you.

4. I can't really claim to be an .... of Frank Sinatra's singing, but I do consider myself an admirer.

5. Hundreds were crushed to death in the ....

6. I think they first imposed a trade .... on Cuba back at the start of the 60s.

7. It's a film that's very much of its time. I mean, it captures the .... of the era perfectly.

8. I'd take what he said with a pinch of salt if I were you. It was just beer and teenage .... talking!

6 | Abbreviations

Match the abbreviations in the box with the descriptions. Two of the abbreviations are based on other languages!

ASAP	IMF	MRSA	NB	PC
CIA	MP	NATO	NGO	RSVP

1. a request for a reply to an invitation ....

2. a politician ....

3. a political ideology ....

4. to show you need something urgently ....

5. a world economic organisation ....

6. something you write when you want the reader to pay special attention to what follows ....

7. charities are an example of this kind of organisation ....

8. a very resistant bug ....

9. an American intelligence organisation ....

10. a military alliance ....

7 | Temperature idioms

Choose the correct word to complete the idioms.

1. I'm just going to *cool off / chill / cool* this weekend and do as little as possible.

2. I thought quitting my job was a good idea last night, but in the *hot / cold / warm* light of day I'm not so sure.

3. Henrik and Bob got into this *hot / warm / heated* discussion about politics and then it just *boiled over / overheated / roasted* into a fight. We had to separate them and give them time to *get cold / cool off / freeze*.

4. When we first proposed setting up a joint venture with another company, the plan got a fairly *cold / warm / hot* reception, but when we got down to details the top management got *icy / chilly / cold* feet and decided to drop the idea.

5. When the government minister addressed the conference, he received quite a *cold / frosty / freezing* reception from the audience, but I have to say I *warmed / heated / cooled* to him as his speech went on. He's quite charismatic.

Use a dictionary to find other idioms with these words:

cold   cool   freeze   hot   warm

8 Collocations

Complete each set of collocations with a noun from the text on page 134 of the Coursebook.

1. .... mark a ~ in attitudes, represent a radical ~ in policy, produce a ~ to the right, a ~ away from centralisation

2. .... loosen your ~, strengthen their ~ on power, have a firm ~ on things, slowly come to ~s with the situation, an iron ~

3. .... the overwhelming ~, there's a silent ~ who oppose the plans, the vast ~ of cases, hold a ~ stake in the company, the ~ view

4. .... be subjected to physical ~, alleged human rights ~s, suffer racial ~, a term of ~, a target of ~, endure verbal ~, hurl ~

5. .... have a policy of zero ~, show remarkable ~ towards their persecutors, have a low ~ to alcohol, learn religious ~

6. .... mouth a ~, bleep out the ~s, use a string of ~s, mutter a ~ under his breath, a mild ~

7. .... uphold a long and noble ~, break with ~, revive an ancient ~, follow a family ~, go against a well-established ~

Underline the collocations that are new for you.

9 Given

Make complete sentences by matching the beginnings and endings.

1. Given the fact she's only been learning for six months, ☐

2. In view of her previous criminal record, ☐

3. Given what we paid for the car, ☐

4. In view of our financial situation this time last year, ☐

5. In view of the state of the house, ☐

a. I think we've made a remarkable recovery.
b. I think an offer of £200,000 is remarkably generous.
c. she's made remarkable progress.
d. I thought they were remarkably lenient.
e. I think it's lasted a remarkably long time.

How many beginnings with *Given* / *In view of* can you think of for these two sentence endings?

• ...., the interview went remarkably well.

• ...., progress was bound to be difficult.

10 Key words for writing: results

Look at these different ways of expressing results.

As a result of / *Because of* / *Due to* the strike, many holidaymakers were stranded at the airport.

The old saying claims that your enemy's enemy is your friend. *Therefore* / *Given this* / *As a result* / *As such* / *Consequently*, an alliance between the two firms is not impossible.

I accidentally pressed the wrong button, *thereby* deleting weeks of work!

Match the sentence beginnings with the endings.

1. This information can then be passed onto future staff, ☐

2. GDP growth accelerated in the last quarter, ☐

3. Sleeping policemen were installed in the area recently, ☐

4. China's consumers are growing richer and more comfortable about taking on debt, ☐

5. Our goal is to create products that enhance the speed, power and performance of IT systems, ☐

a. thereby spurring an expansion of imports.
b. thereby inadvertently exacerbating the already appalling traffic flow.
c. thereby sparking the interest of foreign banks interested in issuing them credit cards.
d. thereby increasing their value to the user.
e. thereby ensuring consistency of practice.

Complete the sentences with the words in the box.

as a result	knock-on effect	therefore
consequently	resulting in	

6. This decision has had an immediate .... on high street prices.

7. .... of government policies, logging will be allowed to continue to blight the rainforest.

8. A witness to the robbery came forward last night. ...., the thieves were arrested within the hour.

9. Sewage leaked into the local river, ... the death of a large number of fish.

10. You only achieved 48 per cent in your recent examination. ...., you will need to resit in September.

24 Celebrity and scandal

1 Describing why people are famous

Complete each description with one of the groups in the box, putting the words in the correct order.

doing + former + embroiled
lay + chequered + maverick
pear-shaped + wrangling + hits
shot + rough + consecutive
stint + launched + lucrative
stir + host + contestants

1. He's a ... cabinet minister who became ... in this big financial scandal. He was accused of corruption and ended up ... six years in jail.

2. She started out in theatre, but then got offered this ... modelling contract. She did a brief ... in Hollywood and has just recently ... her own line of designer jewellery.

3. He ... to fame in the 1980s, winning the World Snooker Championships for three ... years, but he then went completely off the rails and was last seen sleeping ... .

4. She used to be in this girl band which had a few smash ... , but they all fell out and the whole thing went ... . There was an acrimonious split and endless legal ... after that!

5. He used to ... this game show on Channel Nine, but ended up marrying one of the ... . As you can imagine, that caused quite a ... in the press!

6. She's had quite a ... career. She started out as a ... politician, but then got embroiled in a sex scandal. She quit and ... low for a few years, before re-emerging as a campaigner for social justice.

Language note

If you *get / become embroiled*, you become involved in unpleasant situations that can be tricky to get out of.

An *acrimonious split* is unpleasant and involves lots of anger and arguments. The opposite is an *amicable split*.

Things *went pear-shaped* is an informal way of saying things went wrong and ended badly.

If you *have a chequered career*, you *have more than your fair share of ups and downs* – you experience both successes and failures.

2 Key word: *career*

Complete the sentences with the correct form of the verbs in the box.

be dogged	embark	revive	span
carve out	launch	ruin	take off

1. He got a lucky break with a role in this hit movie, and that .... his career.

2. Basically, what the firm needs is highly intelligent, motivated young people who are keen to .... a career for themselves.

3. He was caught kerb-crawling and the ensuing infamy basically .... his career.

4. After graduating, he .... on a career in the oil industry and only retired last year.

5. He had a long and distinguished career in the navy, ... some 35 years.

6. She's had a fairly illustrious career, but one that .... by controversy and incident.

7. She had her first poems published when she was in her 20s, but her career didn't .... until the publication of her third novel.

8. She's basically a glamour model, but she's recently .... a sideline career as a singer as well.

Now complete the sentences with these nouns.

downs	peak	structure
guidance	prospects	ups

9. He's had a chequered career, full of .... and ....

10. I'm doing an MBA next year and that'll hopefully enhance my career .... quite substantially.

11. It's quite a strange story. He had this glittering career and then at the very .... of it, he quit and went to live on an island!

12. I like the work, but there's no clear career .... in the whole field, so it's hard to see how I'll ever get promoted.

13. I drifted around for quite a few years after school. I don't feel like I got much career .... when I was younger.

3 Expressions with *and* and *or*

The order of words in expressions is generally fixed. Decide if the words in these expressions are in the correct order.

1. bright and early	7. pick and choose
2. break or make	8. rightly or wrongly
3. give or take	9. straight and narrow
4. later or sooner	10. swim or sink
5. nothing or all	11. tested and tried
6. outs and ins	12. to and fro

Now complete these sentences with eight of the expressions above.

a. Mr T has produced motivational videos to keep kids who might otherwise fall into crime on the ... .

b. I never do things by halves. It's always ... with me.

c. I don't know all the ... of the situation, all I know is they're not speaking to each other.

d. This is really a ... year for my career. If things don't go well, I might have to consider doing something else.

e. My boss threw me in at the deep end and left me to ... .

f. I work in Germany, but my family lives in the UK. So there's a lot of travelling ... , which is quite wearing.

g. You need to cook it for an hour, ... a few minutes.

h. You should tell them. They're going to find out ... .

4 News headlines

Complete the news headlines with these words.

axed	dumped	haul	quizzed	split
blaze	foiled	probe	sham	weds

1. Pop group to ....

2. Picture exclusive – TV star .... childhood sweetheart

3. Top comedian .... after drugs bust shame

4. .... for another woman

5. Footballer's son kidnap ....

6. Outed! MP's marriage is a ....

7. £100m .... in customs raid

8. Death toll rises from nightclub ....

9. PM orders .... into police abuse allegations

10. Four .... over bomb plot

5 Card-playing idioms

A cabinet *reshuffle* is an example of an idiom from playing cards. Match the meanings with the card-playing idioms.

1. You never know what he's thinking. ☐

2. I wish he'd tell me exactly what he wants. ☐

3. He's not very good at dealing with people. ☐

4. He's not really going to carry out his threat. ☐

5. I didn't think he would, but he's actually done it. ☐

6. He's in a very strong position. ☐

7. I think he's slightly mad. ☐

8. He had a disadvantaged upbringing. ☐

a. He should lay his cards on the table.

b. You should call his bluff.

c. It's not his strong suit.

d. He keeps his cards very close to his chest.

e. He was dealt a poor hand.

f. He's holding all the aces.

g. He's come up trumps.

h. He's not playing with a full deck.

6 Drugs and drug problems

Complete the sentences with these words.

care	habit	relapse
draconian	prescription	shooting up
endemic	rehab	snort

1. Drug use and the attendant problems that go with it has become .... in our society.

2. You sometimes see people .... heroin in the street.

3. Addicts will often .... £1,000 worth of coke a week.

4. Much crime is driven by addicts trying to fund their ....

5. People can sometimes become addicted to .... drugs such as antidepressants and sleeping pills.

6. A lot of drug addicts have grown up in ....

7. Some countries have introduced .... legislation, including the death penalty, to combat the problem.

8. Some people feel addicts should be forced into ....

9. Once out of prison, many addicts .... into addiction.

Writing: Presentations

1 Sample presentation

Complete the text with the words in the box.

aware	contrast	point
bore	expect	position
briefly	forgot	reminds
comprehensive	handout	tight

I'd like to start by saying hi. It's good to see you all and I hope I'm not going to (1) ... you silly over the next 30 minutes! To be honest, half an hour isn't really enough to give a (2) ... picture, but that's the time I've been given. I know you all have a (3) ... schedule today, so I'll try to be as brief as I can.

You are all in the lucky (4) ... of being holiday representatives for Flyus and I know you've already had sessions today on the people and culture of places in Eastern Europe, the Med and Japan. I'm here to take you somewhere a little sunnier – to the Caribbean, and in particular to the island of Barbados.

So, to talk (5) ... about the island itself. Could you all please look at the first set of pictures on your (6) ... ? I'm sure you all know the idyllic picture postcards of the Caribbean, showing white beaches, palm trees and turquoise waters – and yes, it really is like that – but as you can see, different parts of the island have different features. The west coast has a monopoly of quiet empty stretches of beach. In (7) ... , the south is more like the south of Spain – wall-to-wall tourists, bars, restaurants and cheap hotels!

My next (8) ... is that you really need to be (9) ... of the laid-back attitude of most Bajans. This may be charming for tourists, but as holiday reps you'll have to cope with five o'clock being six or even seven, and 'this morning' could well end up being 'this afternoon'. This is true not only when you are trying to book tours, but also in other professional situations. Don't (10) ... to get away with less than an hour in a bank queue! But the Bajans are delightful people. Get to know them – get to know your local characters. It will make your life a damn sight easier.

Oh – I nearly (11) ... – it gets a bit hot over there, so stay out of the midday sun – on your days off, that is! And that (12) ... me – cover yourself with sun screen.

And finally – let me finish by saying – stay well clear of the rum punch if you're working! Otherwise, consume as much as possible in the time you have available! Good luck and have a great time!

2 Register (1)

In many presentations, a friendly tone is preferable to a more formal one. Complete the collocations by adding more formal synonyms.

accelerate	collaborate on	penetrate
amalgamate	consolidate	relocate
calculate	exploit	remunerate
capitalise on	formulate	utilise

1. use / .... new technology
2. move / .... production to China
3. combine / .... the two sets of data
4. pay / .... staff for their hard work
5. strengthen / .... our position
6. speed up / .... the process
7. think up / .... new policies
8. break into / .... new markets
9. work out / .... projected earnings
10. work together on / .... the project
11. make full use of / .... new opportunities
12. take advantage of / .... rivals' weaknesses

3 Register (2)

Rewrite the sentences using the words in brackets so that they are more informal.

1. It is a well-known fact that the English will bet on almost anything! (everybody)
2. It is a little-known fact that 80 per cent of the world's millionaires are self-employed. (lot / people / not realise)
3. It's been shown that in countries where drugs are legal, use drops significantly. (they)
4. It's being suggested that the price war is a consequence of globalisation. (they)
5. It's generally agreed that the rich live longer. (almost everyone)

4 Writing

Write a presentation for holiday representatives about a city or country you know well. Decide first which of the expressions from this page you want to use and how formal/informal you want your presentation to be.

Grammar: Conditionals

1 Introducing a condition

Complete the conversations with the words in the box, all of which introduce conditions.

assuming	had	provided	so long	unless
even if	if only	should	suppose	whether

1. A: I can't believe we lost all that money.

    B: I know! .... we'd backed the favourite to win instead of your boss's horse!

2. We'd like you to start work on Monday – .... you accept the job, of course.

3. A: Can I have Friday night off?

    B: Yeah, ... you can swap your shift.

4. A: You don't think he did it, do you?

    B: Well, let's just .... he did kill her. How would he then have disposed of the body?

5. A: What would you do if you found a wallet?

    B: It'd depend .... it had an address with it or not, to be honest.

    A: Well, suppose it did, what then?

6. A: Can you give me a lift home?

    B: Sure – .... as you don't mind waiting. I've got some things to do before I go back.

7. A: How's the Chinese coming along?

    B: Terrible. I think I'd be struggling with it .... I had three hours of lessons a day.

8. A: You should've asked me. I'm good with cars.

    B: Well, ... I known that, I would've!

9. Nothing gets done around here – .... I do it!

10. .... you require any further information, please do not hesitate to get in touch.

Language note

You can say 'provided you can do it' or 'providing you can do it'. You can also say 'so long as you do it' or 'as long as you do it'. Both expressions mean the same thing.

2 Different kinds of conditional sentences

Make complete conditional sentences by matching the beginnings and the endings.

1. If I tell you to do something, ☐
2. I'll do it ☐
3. If I'd known you were going to be here today, ☐
4. My gran would give us the fiercest of looks ☐
5. If he's not here by now, ☐
6. If you ask me, ☐
7. If you knew him as well as I know him, ☐
8. If you heard the way he talks, ☐
9. If you don't mind, ☐
10. I'd probably be stuck in some dead-end job now ☐

a. you wouldn't have said that.
b. he's a complete waste of space!
c. you do it. Right?
d. if she hadn't encouraged me to better myself.
e. if we ever did anything wrong.
f. you'd think he owned the place!
g. if you'll do it.
h. I'd rather stay in. But you go if you want to.
i. he must've decided to give it a miss. He did say he might.
j. I could've rearranged my schedule and had lunch with you.

Complete these sentences with the verbs in brackets in the most appropriate form.

11. If you ever .... the chance to go skiing, ... You .... it. (get, go, love)

12. Assuming we .... planning permission, the building work .... underway next month. (get, get)

13. Honestly, she's such a busybody! She .... meddling even if she .... (not stop, try)

14. Don't take it personally. If you .... through what he has, you'd .... very angry too. (be, be)

15. I .... you a hand if you .... (give, like)

Word building

Some words are connected by the same root and have different forms as adjectives, verbs or nouns. Sometimes a word class may have more than one form associated with the same word. For example, the adjectives *informed*, *misinformed*, *informative*, *uninformative* all come from the same base word: *inform*.

Words which have the same root may have radically different values in terms of frequency, will generally collocate quite differently, and may even vary in meaning. For example, the adjectives *bored* and *boring* are far more common than the verb *bore*.

Look at the ways these words collocate:

confuse

You're ~ing me, don't ~ the issue, to ~ matters, I think you're ~ing me with someone else

confused

I'm ~, the situation's still very ~, become ~ as she got older

confusing

a very ~ plot, he left a ~ message, his explanation was quite ~

confusion

There's a lot of ~ about the results, the changes have led to a lot of ~, we lost each other in the ~, to avoid any further ~

In the examples above, you can see a connected meaning with all the examples, which is to do with not knowing what's happening or not understanding something. However, a word like *deep* has a number of different meanings and its related words are used in very different circumstances:

deep

the river's quite ~, how ~ is it?, he had a ~ cut, he's got a very ~ voice, take a ~ breath, we had a ~ conversation, he was ~ in conversation, we're in ~ shit!, thrown in at the ~ end

depth

the pool is 3m in ~, she's got hidden ~s (of talent), a great ~ of knowledge, the news isn't covered in great ~, discuss the issue in ~, underestimate the ~ of feeling, in the ~s of depression, come out of the ~s of recession, feel out of my ~

deepen

the recession is ~ing, the conflict has ~ed, the course has ~ed my understanding, the mystery ~s

Notice also that a *deep conversation* is not the same as *discussing* something *in depth*. Something *deep* is serious and philosophical – often about life and death. However, you could discuss or analyse a football game or a recent film *in depth* – you go into a lot of detail – but it's not necessarily profound or serious.

The final thing to note is that while your own language may have equivalent grammatical forms of a word (adjective, noun, etc.), they are likely to be used differently in English.

Organising your study

The following pages provide examples of how you might organise and learn groups of related words.

- The first thing to do is to organise the words starting from the most common keyword which you come across. This might not be the simplest form, as we saw with the word *bored* above. Have one column or page for each letter so that you can add examples as shown with the letters A to B here.
- Another way to organise your learning is to work from common endings such as *-ive*, *-tion*, *-en*. You might start with an example of a word with this ending and then list some of the other forms connected to it.
- You could have pages or columns dedicated to a particular prefix such as *anti-*, *over-*, *hyper-*, etc. Similarly, you could list affixes such as *-ment* and *-ion*.
- Finally, you may have pages dedicated to words that may be confused because they are connected to the same root, or are all adjectives or verbs but have different meanings. For example, *intense*, *intensive* and *intensified* or *demonstrable* and *demonstrative*, *differ* and *differentiate*.

In all cases, it is a good idea to write example collocations or sentences for some or all of the different forms for the reasons outlined above. The following pages show examples of this.

Look through the following pages and see how many collocations are new to you.

Write your own example collocations and sentences.

Use a good English–English dictionary or collocations dictionary such as those in the *Cobuild* series.

A

able

able *don't feel ~ to help, prove to be a very ~ replacement, be hardly ~ to walk, be barely ~ to cope, be perfectly ~ to look after herself*

ability *have the ~ to succeed, demonstrate an artistic ~, lose my ~ to speak, do it to the best of my ~, assess his ~ to do the job, a mixed-~ class*

disabled *the accident left him severely ~, be mentally ~, work with ~ people, a charity for the ~*

disable *press a button to ~ the machine*

enable *a programme to ~ older people to study, insulin ~s the body to store sugar, ~ easier access*

unable *feel ~ to talk about the problem, be either unwilling or ~ to help*

inability *have / overcome an ~ to relate to people*

account

account *give a blow-by-blow ~, a vivid ~, provide a detailed ~, an eyewitness ~, write a clear ~ of the accident, bring him to ~ for his actions, call the government to ~, be held to ~ for the mess, give a good ~ of yourself*

accounts *do the ~, keep the ~ up-to-date, submit my ~ to the tax office, have someone audit the ~*

accountable *be held directly ~ for the disaster, be ~ to the public, he's not ~ for his actions, fully ~ to parliament*

unaccountable *~ bureaucrats, be ruled by an ~ elite, an ~ feeling*

accountability *demand greater ~, financial ~, enhance ~, weaken ~*

accountant *a trainee ~, become a qualified ~, a chartered ~*

accountancy *go into ~, study ~, have a career in ~, join an ~ firm, use creative ~ to hide the losses*

accuse

accuse *falsely ~ her of lying, be ~d of theft, he virtually ~d me of fraud, I'm not ~ing anyone of anything!*

accusation *level a number of ~s against them, deny ~s of corruption, several ~s have been brought against the government, withdraw an accusation, prove an ~, dismiss the ~, groundless ~s, resign amid ~s of fraud*

accused *the ~ stood in the dock, the ~ was cross-examined*

add

add *~ some salt and pepper, ~ a stamp to your collection, ~ a company to your list of clients, ~ and subtract, I should ~, his story doesn't ~ up, ~ on five minutes for injury time, ~ to the confusion, ~ insult to injury*

addition *make valuable ~s to the collection, a new ~ to the team, welcome the latest ~ to the company, in ~*

additional *have an ~ charge, create 20 ~ jobs*

advantage

advantage *take full ~ of the opportunity, be at an ~, his experience gives him an ~ over the other competitors*

disadvantage *weigh up the advantages and ~s, my dyslexia puts me at a ~, the plan actually worked to their ~*

disadvantaged *economically ~, socially ~, ~ areas, help ~ groups*

advantageous *be in an ~ position, the deal is mutually ~, tax breaks are ~ to married couples, find it ~ to wait, prove ~*

B

believe

believe *I don't ~ it, I find that very difficult to ~, I don't ~ a word of it, passionately ~ in a project, ~ in ghosts, if you ~ that, you'll ~ anything, he strongly ~s he's right, ten people are ~d to be dead, the man is ~d to be carrying a gun*

believable *the characters were very ~, her story was(n't) very ~*

unbelievable *Peru was ~, we had an ~ time, the conditions they're working under are ~, the cold was ~, I find it ~ that he would do such a thing, it's ~ that , his story was totally ~*

unbelievably *it's ~ bad, the acting was ~ good, it was an ~ stupid thing to do, it was ~ hot, ~, it actually worked*

belief *have strong ~s, profound ~, an unshakeable ~ in yourself, be persecuted for their religious / political ~s, follow traditional ~s, do it under the mistaken / misguided ~ that, stick to your ~s, (re)affirm your ~, strengthen your ~, contrary to popular ~, have a very fixed set of ~s, his behaviour was completely beyond ~*

disbelief *we watched / stared in complete ~, he expressed utter ~, there was widespread ~ at the claim, you need to suspend your ~, she couldn't hide her ~*

believer *I'm a fervent / great ~ in the benefits of exercise, she's a passionate ~ in what she's doing, he's a true ~*

bitter

bitter *have a slightly ~ taste, be involved in a ~ dispute, she feels very ~ about her divorce, he's very ~, the affair left a ~ taste in the mouth, failing was a ~ disappointment, I'm speaking from ~ experience, we kept going till the ~ end, it's ~ weather*

bitterly *we were ~ disappointed by the result, they complained ~, the proposal has been ~ opposed, it's ~ cold outside*

bitterness *the strike has caused a lot of ~, she's shown no ~ towards her attacker, there's a lot of ~ among teachers over the pay deal, the lemon gives it a hint of ~*

bomb

bomb *there's been a ~ explosion, several people died in the ~ blast, a ~ went off in the city centre, the ~ caused extensive damage, there was a ~ scare in the train station, the army detonated the ~ in a controlled explosion, ~ disposal experts, they're trying to develop a nuclear ~, it must've cost a ~*

bomb (v) *the city was heavily ~ed during the war, terrorists ~ed the market, the air force carpet-~ed the area, the car was absolutely ~ing down the street*

bombing *there has been a spate of ~s, security's been tightened since the ~, several people have died in a suicide ~, the army has been accused of using indiscriminate ~*

bomber *police have caught the ~s, be attacked by a suicide ~*

bombard *the city was heavily ~ed for weeks, the government's been ~ed with criticism, the company was ~ed with complaints, we're constantly ~ed with advertising*

bombardment *the city has come under heavy ~, the town has withstood intense ~ for several months, survive a ~, cease their ~, launch an aerial ~, be killed during the ~*

Adjective endings

abrasive *be an ~ character, have an ~ manner, have an ~ surface*
abrasiveness, abrasion

active *try and keep ~, remain ~ in old age, be ~ in the church, be an ~ member of a group, have ~ talks to solve the dispute, take ~ steps to calm the situation, politically ~, sexually ~, a highly ~ volcano*
inactive, actively, activity, action, activist, activism, activate

aggressive *become extremely ~, be openly ~, control ~ behaviour, ~ questioning of a witness, launch an ~ campaign, suffer from an ~ disease, an ~ treatment plan*
aggressively, aggression, aggressor

appreciative *be very ~, give ~ applause, an ~ smile*
appreciated, appreciable, appreciation, appreciate, appreciatively

captive *take someone ~, hold them ~ for days, keep animals ~ in a zoo, have a ~ audience*
a captive, captivity, capture (v, n), captivate, captivating

competitive *be fiercely ~, take part in ~ sport, be in a ~ market, have a ~ edge, try and remain ~, a ~ pricing policy*
competing, competitiveness, competition, competitor, compete

decisive *he's (not) very ~, the move proved ~, play a ~ role in the negotiations, be a ~ factor, take ~ action on global warming, take a ~ step towards further integration, win a ~ victory, a ~ battle*
decisiveness, indecisive, indecision, indecisiveness, decisively, indecisively, decision, decided, undecided, decide

definitive *write the ~ work on the subject, read the ~ biography of Churchill, give a ~ answer, announce / sign a ~ agreement, make a ~ statement, give a ~ version of events*
definite, definitely, definitively, definition, define

defensive *he can get very ~ about it, take up a ~ position, take ~ measures, a ~ team, be on the ~, forced onto the ~*
defensiveness, defensively, defence, defenceless, (in)defensible, defend, defender, defendant

formative *Picasso spent his ~ years in Barcelona, a ~ influence in the development of a child, in / during the ~ years, the ~ years of the United States*
formation, form(n, v), format (n, v), (in)formal, (in)formality, formalise

Some other *-ive* adjectives

alternative, apprehensive, comprehensive, constructive, creative, destructive, effective, excessive, imaginative, intensive, lucrative, massive, offensive, productive, protective, qualitative, restrictive, secretive, tentative

Other adjective suffixes you might look at

-able *(dis)agreeable, applicable, bankable, (un)beatable, (un)believable, (un)breakable, (in)calculable, creditable, demonstrable, (un)doable, (un)enviable, (un)fashionable, (dis)honourable, (in)hospitable, knowledgeable, memorable, (im)passable, (un)profitable, regrettable, (in)tolerable*

-al *alphabetical, clerical, (hyper)critical, medical, medicinal, (un)musical, philosophical, (a)political, psychological, (im)practical, theatrical, triumphal*

-ible *(in)accessible, (in)comprehensible, (in)credible, deductible, (in)defensible, divisible, permissible, (im)possible, (ir)resistible*

-ic *acidic, (non-)alcoholic, (in)artistic, (un)charismatic, (un)characteristic, climactic, (un)diplomatic, (un)democratic, energetic, enthusiastic, heroic, idiotic, ironic, magnetic, optimistic, patriotic, pedantic, poetic, (un)realistic, symbolic, sympathetic, (un)systematic, xenophobic*

-ish *amateurish, babyish, biggish, bluish, darkish, feverish, greenish, hawkish, Jewish, Kurdish, longish, oldish, peckish, reddish, slavish, snobbish, Swedish, tallish, ticklish, warmish, youngish*

-ful *boastful, cheerful, deceitful, dutiful, forceful, graceful, harmful, joyful, merciful, playful, shameful, tactful, thankful, useful, woeful, youthful*

Some words ending in *-ful* are nouns, not adjectives: *armful, bucketful, cupful, handful, mouthful, roomful, spoonful*

-less *airless, brainless, countless, childless, endless, fearless, flawless, gutless, harmless, heartless, humourless, lawless, lifeless, meaningless, motionless, priceless, powerless, restless, seedless, speechless, spotless, tactless, timeless, thankless, useless, windless*

A few words ending in *-less* are adverbs, not adjectives. For example: *doubtless, regardless*

-ous *(dis)advantageous, (un)ambiguous, (in)cautious, contemptuous, continuous, enormous, furious, gorgeous, gracious, humorous, impetuous, jealous, luminous, (un)nutritious, obvious, religious, simultaneous, spacious, suspicious, tenacious, ubiquitous, various, virtuous*

-y *blotchy, bulky, bushy, cloudy, dusty, fatty, flowery, grassy, hairy, itchy, jammy, kinky, leafy, muddy, nutty, oily, picky, quivery, rusty, sketchy, sneaky, stumpy, tinny, wintry, worthy*

Remember – learning individual words and meanings is only part of the story! You need to learn the collocations and typical grammar these words are used with.

Noun endings

assassination *plot an ~, survive an ~ attempt, a character ~*
assassin, assassinate, to be assassinated

attention *she always has to be the centre of ~, attract
international ~, pay scant ~ to the problem, recent events
have focused ~ on the matter, try to divert ~ away from the
matter, have a short ~ span*
attend to, attentive, attentively

conversation *get into a ~ with someone, try to make ~, the
subject cropped up in a ~, a very one-sided ~, he dominates
the ~, his only topic of ~ is golf, the art of ~*
conversationalist, converse, conversational,
conversationally

conviction *secure a ~, appeal against a ~, uphold the appeal
against a ~, overturn the ~, have three previous ~s, the ~
was declared unsafe, the ~ rate is very low*
convict, convict, to be convicted of a crime, convicted

compensation *be eligible for ~, receive adequate ~, be
awarded ~, receive full ~, be refused ~, pay £10,000 in ~, file
a ~ claim*
compensate, compensatory

corruption *~ is rife, widespread ~, rampant ~, high-level ~ ,
expose ~, curb ~, tackle ~, root out ~, face allegations of ~,
be embroiled in a ~ scandal*
corrupt, to be corrupted, corruptible, incorruptible,
incorruptibility, corruptly

demonstration *stage a ~, mass ~s against the war, gather
for a peaceful ~, spontaneous ~s, a violent ~, disperse the ~,
the ~ degenerated into a full-scale riot* demonstrator,
demonstrate, demonstrative, undemonstrative,
demonstratively

discrimination *racial ~, widespread sexual ~, overt religious
~, blatant ~, positive ~, institutionalised ~, suffer ~, fight ~, ~
on the grounds of old age*
discriminate, to be discriminated against, discriminatory

Some other -ion nouns

*action, addition, beautification, collection, combination,
contribution, creation, decision, direction, distribution, education,
examination, explanation, formation, gratification, isolation,
limitation, motivation, nation, nutrition, operation, organisation,
perception, permission, persecution, possession, prescription,
protection, reaction, realisation, reduction, reputation, seduction,
simulation, taxation, transformation, victimisation*

Other noun suffixes you might look at

-ance *abundance, advance, allowance, (dis)appearance,
annoyance, balance, brilliance, distance, dominance,
extravagance, furtherance, ignorance, importance, insurance,
pittance, (ir)relevance, reluctance, resistance, (in)significance,
surveillance, (in)tolerance*

-dom *freedom, martyrdom, officialdom, stardom, wisdom*

-ence *absence, adolescence, coherence, coincidence, confidence,
convenience, defence, dependence, emergence, existence,
experience, incidence, indulgence, influence, interference,
(dis)obedience, indifference, (im)patience, persistence,
presence, recurrence, residence, silence, violence*

-er *bouncer, character, computer, danger, disorder, explorer,
foreigner, government minister, leader, loser, painter, rapper,
reader, speaker, teacher, winner*

-hood *childhood, fatherhood, motherhood, neighbourhood*

-ism *ageism, consumerism, euphemism, heroism, multi-racialism,
plagiarism, racism, sexism, symbolism, tourism*

-ist *fascist, publicist, racist, realist, self-publicist, terrorist*

-ity *activity, authority, celebrity, criminality, disability, diversity,
eternity, ferocity, incredulity, intensity, majority, minority,
popularity, publicity, reality, (in)sanity, scarcity, security,
sexuality, tranquillity*

-ment *achievement, acknowledgement, (dis)agreement,
appointment, argument, attachment, commitment,
containment, deployment, endorsement, environment,
excitement, government, improvement, investment,
involvement, management, payment, punishment,
replacement, retirement, statement, treatment*

-ness *aggressiveness, awkwardness, awareness, bitterness,
blindness, carelessness, consciousness, drunkenness,
effectiveness, friendliness, happiness, illness, laziness,
loneliness, madness, openness, political correctness, rudeness,
sickness, tenderness, ugliness, weakness*

-or *actor, creator, dictator, director, doctor, eco-warrior, lowest
common denominator, professor, survivor*

-ship *friendship, censorship, leadership, ownership*

Verb endings

brighten *the weather might ~ up, that's ~ed up my day, ~ the
room*
bright, brightness, brightly

broaden *~ your horizons, travel ~s the mind, his smile ~ed*
broad, breadth, broadly

darken *the sky's beginning to ~, his mood ~ed with the news,
never ~ my door again!*
dark, darkened, darkness, the dark, darkly

deaden *take an aspirin to ~ the pain, cover it to ~ the noise*
dead, death, the dead, deadly, die

deafen *be almost ~ed by the noise, you almost ~ed me!*
deaf, deafness, the deaf, deafening

deepen *the recession is ~ing, the conflict has ~ed, the course
has ~ed my understanding, the mystery ~s, ~ the channel*
deep, depth, deeply

flatten *the town was ~ed during the war, he nearly ~ed me,
prices are beginning to ~ out*
flat, flattened, flatness, flatly

heighten *~ awareness of the problem, the reviews ~ed
expectations, ~ security, smoking ~s the risk of getting cancer*
high, height, heightened, highly

lighten *the new staff have ~ed my workload, measures aimed
at ~ing the tax burden on small businesses, ~ the colour of
my hair, he managed to ~ the mood, ~ up and stop taking
everything so seriously!*
light, lightness, lightly

quieten *can everyone ~ down, the crowd ~ed, hopefully things
will ~ down at work*
quiet, quiet (n, v) quietly, disquiet

strengthen *work to ~ the bridge, do exercises to ~ your back / muscles, Barcelona have ~ed their team, the evidence will ~ their case, ~ your belief, the news only ~ed his resolve, the wind has ~ considerably, his position in the party has ~ed, the pound's ~ against the euro*
strong, strongly, strength

Some other *-en* verbs

blacken, cheapen, dampen, fatten, freshen (up), harden, lengthen, lessen, loosen, moisten, sharpen, shorten, sicken, stiffen, straighten, sweeten, thicken, tighten, toughen, weaken, widen, worsen

Some other verb affixes you might look at

-ate *accumulate, animate, communicate, compensate, complicate, decimate, delineate, dictate, duplicate, emigrate, evaporate, exacerbate, fixate, generate, immigrate, implicate, interrogate, investigate, (re)invigorate, legislate, (re)locate, migrate, motivate, speculate*

em- *embark, embed, embitter, embody, empower*

en- *enable, encase, encircle, enclose, encourage, endanger, endear, enfold, (dis)enfranchise, engulf, enjoy, enlarge, enlist, enrage, enrich, entrench, entrust*

-ify *amplify, beautify, clarify, classify, dignify, diversify, falsify, glorify, gratify, horrify, identify, intensify, justify, magnify, modify, notify, purify, qualify, satisfy, signify, simplify, solidify, specify, testify, terrify*

-ise / -ize *apologise, authorise, characterise, colonise, criticise, economise, emphasise, epitomise, equalise, fantasise, glamorise, harmonise, hospitalise, hypothesise, jeopardise, legalise, legitimise, memorise, modernise, moralise, neutralise, pressurise, publicise, rationalise, revolutionise, stabilise, standardise, subsidise, summarise, symbolise, sympathise, terrorise, victimise, visualise*

Real English

In British English we prefer to use **-ise**, whereas in American English the preference is **-ize**. Choose whichever you prefer! However, note that some verbs are spelt with **-ise** in both forms of English. For example: *advise, comprise, compromise, surprise.*

Confusing words

Notice that sometimes words with similar meanings – like those below – may share some collocations and be synonymous in some situations. However, there will always be some collocations that are particular to one word, but not the other(s). Hence, the best way to distinguish them is to do something like this!

continual *be in ~ pain, live in ~ fear of arrest, suffer ~ harassment, be a ~ problem, be sick of the ~ arguments*

continually *argue ~, new products ~ come on the market, be ~ interrupted, be ~ changing their ideas, a process of ~ updating the system, pick on me ~*

continued (or continuing) *thanks for your ~ support, there's been ~ fighting today, there's ~ opposition to the proposals, ~ involvement, ~ interest*

continuous *be a ~ process, have a ~ supply of water, there's ~ noise outside, ~ assessment, be in ~ employment, come under ~ attack, a ~ flow of people, a ~ line of traffic, a ~ source of inspiration*

continuously *rain ~ for ten days, speak ~ for an hour, work here ~ since 1992*

intense *he's in ~ pain, survive the ~ cold / heat, generate ~ interest, have an ~ dislike of, have ~ competition, there's been ~ speculation, he's very ~ about everything*

intensive *do an ~ course, have ~ training, be in ~ care, hold ~ negotiations, conduct an ~ investigation, ~ farming, capital-~, a very labour-~ industry*

legalise *campaign to ~ euthanasia, campaign against ~ing drugs, some countries have ~d gay marriage*

legislate *~ to protect people's right, ~ on file-sharing, ~ to outlaw age discrimination, you can't ~ for these things / bad luck*

motive *have an ulterior ~ for helping, act from pure ~s, have a strong ~, there's no clear ~ for the attack, police try and establish a ~, the crime had a racial ~, I question his ~s for marrying her*

motivation *have a strong ~ to succeed, my main ~ for doing the course, have no ~, there's a lack of ~ among the staff, I lost my ~, the underlying ~ behind the action*

variable *his films are of ~ quality, the speed's ~, ~ weather conditions, infinitely ~ possibilities*

various *come in ~ shapes and sizes, there are ~ possibilities, ~ ways of doing it, for ~ reasons*

varied *there's a wide and ~ selection, a full and ~ life, a very ~ experience, the food's wonderfully ~, an incredibly ~ country*

This page is for your own notes.

Answer Key

1 Describing people

I 1. tight-fisted + recycles 2. laid-back + loses 3. know-all + knows 4. egomaniac + power 5. fancies + leave 6. whinger + petty 7. slob + lifts 8. push + intimidating

2 1. uncaring 2. disrespectful 3. disinclined 4. unsociable 5. inarticulate 6. dislikeable 7. impatient 8. incompetent 9. uncooperative 10. indecisive

3 1. disrespectful 2. incompetent 3. uncooperative 4. inarticulate 5. uncaring 6. disinclined 7. dislikeable 8. indecisive 9. unsociable 10. impatient
a. dirt b. rid c. painfully d. strikes e. thoroughly f. work

4 1. quite 2. such a 3. not that 4. so 5. a bit of a 6. such a 7. a real 8 not really all that

5 1. neck 2. back 3. face 4. head 5. chest, shoulder 6. eyes

6 1. People here tend to stick together in times of trouble.
2. I didn't manage to stick to the diet in the end.
3. If you stick at it, I'm sure you'll get better.
4. I got stuck next to this nutter on the bus.
5. We should stick some of these photos in an album.
6. It broke but I managed to stick it back together with sellotape.
7. She's stuck in a dead-end job.
8. Just stick your bags in the corner for the moment.
9. Your label's sticking out at the back of your jumper.
10. A lot of people were complaining about the teacher, but I stuck up for her.
11. Are you going to stick around after the class?
12. His teeth stick out a bit.
13. I wish I hadn't put my suit on because I really stuck out like a sore thumb.
14. Nobody really sticks to the speed limit.
15. I'm stuck on this question.
16. She's very stuck in her own way of doing things.

7 1. privileged 2. religious 3. eclectic 4. acquired 5. damaged 6. developing 7. bend 8. flout 9. boosted 10. pursue

8 1. They are forever messing about.
2. He kept going on about his new girlfriend.
3. He won't sit still for a second. He's constantly fidgeting.
4. All he (ever) does is study.
5. The only thing they did was whinge.
6. She's a complete bimbo. All she ever does is paint her nails and try to look beautiful.

9 1. was wondering 2. was (constantly) droning on 3. was fiddling, 's been winding (me) up 4. 's (just) being 5. 've been studying

10 1. after, subsequently 2. afterwards 3. after 4. following 5. Following/After, subsequently 6. following/after, subsequently, afterwards 7. Following, After, Subsequently

2 Work and office politics

I 1. tell + leave 2. broach + catch 3. discuss + end up 4. say + take 5. confront + deny 6. own up + lose

2 1. Physically 2. incredibly/indescribably 3. deadly 4. immensely 5. Financially 6. highly 7. politically 8. academically

3 1. make, decision 2. do, business 3. make, note 4. make, sacrifices 5. do, tax return 6. make, contacts 7. do, study 8. do, accounts 9. make, changes 10. do, photocopying

4 1. where 2. what 3. why 4. how 5. what 6. whether/if

5 1. adapt 2. mince 3. hurtful 4. favourites 5. raving 6. disturbing 7. gets on, chase 8. goes
approachable – 6. conscientious – 7. direct – 2. domineering – 8. even-handed – 4. inflexible – 1. insensitive – 3. moody – 5.

6 1. modest, meet 2. ambitious, exceed 3. carefully, principal 4. long-term, achieving 5. short 6. deliberately 7. legitimate 8. hit, soft 9. intended 10. off

Writing: Punctuation and spelling

2 1. If I were you, I'd learn how to use commas properly.
2. correct
3. Your manager told me, and I quote, 'If you don't like it, you know where the door is!'
4. He's a lovely guy – very easy-going.
5. Writing which is badly punctuated is often taken as a sign of ignorance.
6. I feel I am suitable for the post for a variety of reasons: I have ten years experience in the field; I possess the relevant qualifications; and I am keen to extend my horizons.
7. correct
8. Admittedly, I was partly to blame, but I still feel I was slightly hard done by.
9. correct
10. correct

3 1. independent 2. separate 3. environment 4. calendar 5. correct 6. development 7. receive 8. exaggerated 9. correct 10. correct 11. grammar 12. tendency 13. weird 14. fulfilment (Br English; fulfillment = US English) 15. correct 16. attributes 17. privileged 18. correct 19. accommodation 20. correct

3 Describing places

I 1. no-go 2. dead 3. skyline 4. deprived/run-down, slums 5. remote/isolated, anywhere, scenery 6. sprawling 7. outskirts/edge, shanty town 8. widespread

2 1. number 2. amount, would, was/is 3. more/less, expecting/hoping 4. expectations, turned 5. live/come, actually 6. be, was/is 7. at, to 8. hype, much

3 1. I was/am amazed at how cheap everything was/is.
2. I was/am shocked at the amount of poverty everywhere.
3. I was/am surprised at how easy it was/is to get around.

4. We were/are shocked by the number of crashed cars by the side of the road.
5. I think they were/are expecting (something) better than it actually was/is.
6. It turned out to be far more crowded than we thought (it would be).
7. We thought we would enjoy it more than we actually did.
8. I was expecting (it to be) a disaster, but it turned out to be brilliant.

4 1. gain 2. reverse 3. take 4. attract 5. enter into
6. cause 7. bow to 8. reject

5 1. nowhere 2. miles 3. times 4. league 5. comparison
6. tenfold 8. compared

6 1. enjoyed 2. emerged, handful 3. peak, petered out
4. infighting 5. momentum 6. criticised

7 1. demonstrators, demonstration 2. deprived, deprivation
3. attendance, attended, attendance 4. publicists, publicity
5. indecision, decisively, decision 6. beneficial, beneficiaries

8 2. photographer 3. photogenic 4. economy
5. economist 6. economical 7. technician 8. technicality
9. technical 10. permit (v) 11. permit (n)
12. impermissible

9 1. has been dogged 2. put forward, was (roundly) ejected
3. be seen 4. has attracted/is attracting 5. has
erupted/erupted 6. has provoked/provoked 7. (to)
foster 8. detract 9. repair 10. have started/started/are
starting etc.
a. roundly b. source c. attention d. factions e. on
f. issue

10 1. prior 2. moment 3. preceding 4. due 5. Following
6. subsequently 7. previous 8. subsequent
9 Prior to selling the farm, they had been having problems.
10. Following on from his appearance in a reality TV show,
he received many offers of work.
11. Subsequent to an initial exploratory dig, excavations
revealed/were carried out that revealed the
foundations of an ancient city.
12. Preceding my move to Leeds in 2004, I had held
various posts in the Economics department at the
University of Dundee.

4 | The law

1 1. stands 2. required 3. breakdown 4. lawless, above
5. introduce, offence 6. uphold, taking 7. unenforceable
8. relaxing 9. tightening 10. banning, flouting

2 1. e. 2. b. 3. d. 4. f. 5. c. 6. a.
7. to set the record straight 8. to top it all off 9. To tell
you the truth 10. to say the least 11. to cut a long story
short 12. to add insult to injury

3 1. resort 2. commit 3. charge 4. fight 5. exploit 6. file
7. take 8. guard 9. conduct 10. be awarded 11. infringe
12. introduce
heinous crime, high legal fees, legal battle, custody battle,
new laws, stringent safety rules
file for, resort to, guard against

4 1. completed, purchase 2. regret, resulted 3. previously,
matter 4. refer to, overleaf 5. are advised to, be directed

5 1. must've/must have reminded 2. couldn't/could not get
3. must've/must have been 4. could've/could have throttled
5. would've/would have left 6. should 7. will

8. 'd/would be 9. couldn't/could not believe
10. must've/must have walked 11. could serve
12. would've/would have carried on 13. can imagine
14. would've/would have done
15. could've/could have been

6 1. liability 2. responsibility 3. hypocrite 4. gratitude
5. depth 6. litigation 7. disability 8. immorality

▍ Writing: Letters of application

1 1. recruitment 2. currently 3. role 4. possess
5. interpersonal 6. teamwork 7. committed 8. extend
9. reputation 10. wish

2 1. deputy 2. Prior 3. licence 4. progression 5. hold
6. challenges 7. relevant 8. enclosed

3 1. response 2. suitable, number 3. Should, supply/provide
4. wish, hesitate 5. available, earliest 6. time
7. hearing

▍ Grammar: Time adverbials

1 1. 'd/had built up 2. 've/have got 3. 'll/will have done
4. hasn't/has not made up 5. 've/have received 6. 've/have
spoken 7. 'd/had handed in 8. 'd/had said, 'd/had put
9. have deteriorated
1. By the time (I finished university) 2. by now 3. by
Friday 4. by next week 5. Once 6. As soon as
7. as soon as 8. As soon as 9. Over the past few years

2 1. was working 2. 'll/will be sunning 3. were looking up,
're/are fighting 4. are facing up/have been facing up
5. 're/are teaching 6. wasn't/was not looking

3 1. these days, in my day/when I was a girl 2. there and then
3. on the day 4. To begin with/At first, before long
5. in one moment/shortly 6. at last/in the end
7. At last/Finally, long/a long time, in time 8. the day after
9. currently, in the near future/someday soon 10. Up until
recently/Up until now

5 | Food

1 Fruits: date, fig, nectarine, pomegranate
Herbs: dill, oregano, sage, thyme
Spices: cinnamon, cloves, cumin, turmeric
Vegetables: fennel, parsnip, radish, turnip

2 1. slice 2. warm 3. Sprinkle 4. coat 5. squeeze 6. pour
7. Stir 8. simmer 9. evaporates 10. serve

3 1. g. 2. c. 3. f. 4. a. 5. d. 6. b. 7. h. 8. e.

4 1. lethargic 2. fad, stick to 3. religiously, stink, wind
4. wheat-free 5. crash, shed, piled

5 1. pinch 2. drop 3. hint 4. spoonful 5. slice 6. bite
7. drag 8. sip

6 1. pinch 2. nick 3. host 4. bags 5. floods
6. miscarriages 7. string 8. grain 9. a spate 10. line

7 1. regard/see/view 2. been 3. both 4. to 5. by 6. face
7. no/little 8. approval 9. far 10. demand/need 11. on
12. about/over 13. that 14. covered
15. soon/eventually/well 16. into 17. outweigh
18. otherwise 19. provide/supply 20. season
rigorously tested, potentially dangerous, thoroughly
scrutinised

big business, widespread opposition, positive impact
pollinate (wild) plants, are pandering to (the) demands of,
(huge) swathes of land are covered in plastic, exhaust the
land, benefits outweigh the drawbacks, create jobs

8 1. cake   2. icing   3. cakes   4. bread   5. breadline   6. butter
7. salt   8. eggs
a. butter him up   b. bread and butter   c. a piece of cake
d. on the breadline   e. take it with a pinch of salt

9 1. in   2. with   3. not   4. as   5. order   6. not
7. They tabled the amendment with the sole purpose of
bringing down the government.
8. Please arrive promptly at 2.30 so as not to waste time.
9. Language students should ideally read a great deal in
order to extend their vocabulary.
10. Please come to the police station tomorrow afternoon
in order to complete your statement.
11. We should eat less fat so as to reduce cholesterol and
the dangers of a heart attack.

6 Disasters

1 1. rainfall   2. drop   3. lows   4. famine   5. harvest   6. crops
7. plagues   8. rationed   9. blanket   10. airlift   11. raging
12. bring   13. stretched   14. evacuated   15. charred
16. razed   17. sparked   18. suspicion

2 1. The main suspect is thought to be English.
2. The disease is believed to be a mutant form of horse
influenza.
3. Fifty people are feared to have died in the landslide.
4. Mitchell has (long) been suspected of involvement in
organised crime (for a long time).
5. Darin is reported to have been driving at over a hundred
miles an hour when the accident occurred.
6. The date is not expected to be announced for another
few weeks.
7. The fires are not thought to have been started
deliberately.
8. Dr Kirkland is alleged not to have obtained consent from
his patients to use them in a drug trial.

3 1. blown off   2. sucked up   3. held up   4. run over
5. broken into   6. mugged   7. expelled, caught

4 1. whose   2. order   3. capable   4. donor   5. making
6. range   7. from   8. lack   9. away   10. short   11. aware
12. for   13. signatures
a. provide   b. fund   c. raise   d. undergo   e. escape
f. lobby   g. distribute   h. complete   i. main   j. mobile
k. remote   l. private   m. corporate   n. disadvantaged
o. sexual

5 2a. alleges/alleged   2b. allegation   3a. denial   3b. denied
4a. refused   4b. refusal   5a. persuasion   5b. persuade
6a. reassurance   6b. reassured   7a. approval   7b. approve
8a. accused   8b. accusation   9a. recommended/have
recommended   9b. recommendations

Writing: Discursive essays

1 1. c.   2. a.   3. c.   4. b.   5. a.   6. d.   7. b.   8. a.   9. a.   10. d.

2 1. standpoints   2. impose   3. object, grounds   4. ignited
5. matters   6. evidence   7. cite   8. raises   9. lies

7 Hair and beauty

1 1. e.   2. c.   3. d.   4. f.   5. b.   6. a.

7 7. was/were (both are possible, but *was* is more common in
informal spoken English)   8. wasn't/weren't   9. 'd/had said
10. wouldn't do   11. hadn't told   12. didn't have
13. 'd/would (actually) get, lose

2 1. greying, wrinkled   2. beer gut   3. pierced   4. nicotine-
stained   5. delicate   6. piercing   7. bloodshot, bags
8. boyish   9. stumpy, slender   10. soulful   11. stubble
12. patch, receding   13. cheekbones

3 1. stomach + rumbling   2. stretch + legs   3. eyes +
watering   4. biting + nails   5. wipe + feet   6. back + went

4 1. eye   2. brains, mind   3. muscle   4. arm   5. face
6. blood   7. guts   8. ear

5 1. to have my teeth straightened   2. having my teeth
cleaned, to have it done   3. had/had had/'d had my wisdom
teeth taken out   4. 's/has had her ears pinned back
5. having the house redecorated   6. having her tongue
pierced   7. did (you) have your hair cut, have a bit more
taken off

6 1. affordable   2. frowned upon, Increasing   3. incurable
4. reconstructive   5. creative, dependable, unobtainable

7 1. internationally   2. blissfully   3. clinically   4. surgically
5. outrageously   6. strictly   7. socially   8. bitterly
9. hugely   10. uniquely

8 1. there and then   2. bright and early   3. touch and go
4. to-ing and fro-ing   5. trial and error   6. pros and cons
7. sick and tired   8. cut and dried   9. tried and tested
10. few and far   11. now and again   12. first and foremost

9 1. <u>very</u> heated <u>indeed</u>   2. <u>very</u> cautiously <u>indeed</u>   3. <u>very</u>
important <u>indeed</u>   4. <u>very</u> promising <u>indeed</u>   5. <u>very</u>
seriously <u>indeed</u>   6. <u>very</u> thoroughly <u>indeed</u>   7. <u>very</u> rare
<u>indeed</u>   8. <u>very</u> accurately <u>indeed</u>

8 Politics and elections

1 1. opposition   2. main   3. landslide   4. hung   5. coalition
6. rigging   7. boycotted   8. dictatorship   9. policies
10. dictatorship   11. parliament   12. coalition   13. party
14. election   15. government   16. election
17. government

2 1. d.   2. g.   3. b.   4. a.   5. h.   6. f.   7. c.   8. e.

3 1. charismatic   2. down-to-earth   3. passionate   4. direct
5. shifty   6. spark   7. hypocrite   8. flustered

4 2. What worries me is the lack of investment in education.
3. What (really) disturbs me is the enormous amount of
money they've been ploughing into nuclear weapons.
4. What pleased me was the fact that the guy actually took
responsibility for the cock-up and resigned.
5. What concerns me is the proposal to introduce trial
without jury.
6. What scares me is that this mistake wasn't an isolated
incident.
7. What really angers me is that he speaks down to people
all the time.

5 1. election   2. unelectable   3. electoral   4. elected
5. electorate, re-elected   6. electioneering, electoral
7. election   8. elective

6 1. crack, fell   2. got, confidence   3. stormy, disrupted
4. run-up, local, rig   5. adopted, aimed   6. divided,
differences

7 1. education 2. pensions 3. abortion 4. drugs 5. foreign policy
verb–noun: introduce a national curriculum, increase parental choice, extend the retirement age, force companies to … , take a hard line on … , toughen the law, increase prison sentences, put up trade barriers, withdraw from international agreements
adjective–noun: national curriculum, a confused stance, a far too liberal stance, an isolationist stance, parental choice, higher contributions, a hard line, international agreements
noun–noun: school selection, retirement age, prison sentences, trade barriers

Writing: Essay introductions

1 1. seen 2. vast 3. unthinkable 4. sinister 5. pose 6. becoming 7. address 8. whether 9. concerned

2 1. of 2. in 3. to 4. out 5. about/over 6. with 7. to 8. in

3 1. an increasing 2. a growing 3. quoted 4. thought 5. not concerned 6. goal

Grammar: Continuous forms

1 1. 've/have been trying, 's/is taking 2. 'll/will have been working 3. 'd/had been crying 4. 's/is (forever) going through, 's/is doing, 's/is cleaning up 5. 'll/will have been living 6. 's/is (just) being 7. 've/have been waiting 8. was (just) standing, minding 9. 'd/had been raining, was (just) starting, was (only) doing

2 1. you're twisting what I said 2. it's driving me round the bend 3. I've been tearing my hair out 4. he's always throwing his weight around 5. we're gaining ground on our competitors 6. I'm just feeling a bit under the weather 7. we're just keeping our heads above water

3 1. have been leaking 2. 've/have been sitting 3. be worrying 4. be using, be working 5. be trying 6. 've/have been eavesdropping 8. have been going

4 1. been going 2. hadn't been enjoying, just decided 3. been seeing, trusted 4. I'd been toying, did, helped 5. had 6. was actually just thinking of 7. tried

9 The weather and the environment

1 1. glorious 2. topping 3. turned 4. chill 5. corner 6. dire 7. bucketed down 8. gale 9. fog 10. hailstorm 11. scorching 12. unbearable 13. humidity 14. pig 15. muggy 16. torrential

2 1. f. 2. d. 3. e. 4. c. 5. h. 6. b. 7. g. 8. a.

3 1. impossible 2. unusual 3. unexpected 4. unlike 5. dissimilar 6. unhappy

4 1. lost in the mists of time 2. received a flood of complaints 3. killing this guy in a hail of bullets 4. buried beneath an avalanche of information 5. the winds of change have started blowing 6. a cloud of suspicion still hangs over him 7. living under a cloud of depression 8. greeted by a storm of protest

5 1. weather 2. breezing 3. clouded 4. cloud 5. warm 6. under 7. stormed 8. frosty

6 1. raining + pissing 2. rain + spitting 3. downpour + soaked 4. Chilly + bitter 5. weird + warming 6. stuffy + sauna 7. forecast + miserable 8. draught + heating

7 1. environmentalist, environmentally 2. commercially, commercial 3. assumption, assuming 4. subsidised, subsidisation 5. renewable, renewed 6. destruction, destructive 7. permission, permissive 8. consumption, consumers

8 1. doubt 2. effect 3. no/less 4. hand 5. layer 6. caps 7. very 8. to 9. far 10. while/whereas 11. focus 12. rain 13. due/owing 14. extreme 15. order 16. size 17. causing 18. do

9 1. regarding 2. respect 3. refer 4. d. 5. c. 6. a. 7. b. 8. e. 9. to 10. with 11. of 12. to

10 Shopping

1 1. smuggle 2. dent 3. claim 4. uncover 5. cast 6. launch 7. remain 8. drain 9. undercut 10. introduce

2 1. layout 2. handover 3. breakdown 4. walkout 5. passer-by 6. upbringing

3 1. drop 2. trickle 3. stream 4. flood 5. floodgates 6. wave

4 1. g. 2. b. 3. c. 4. e. 5. d. 6. h. 7. f. 8. a.

5 1. flimsy + sturdy 2. revealing + imagination 3. frumpy + gran 4. tacky + nasty 5. stumpy + slender 6. extravagant + splash out 7. loud + bright 8. clash + place
birthday card – 4. lamp – 8. cardigan – 3. tight jeans – 5. dangly earrings – 6. skimpy dress – 2. table – 1. flowery shirt – 7.

6 1. it's the tip of the iceberg
2. it was the final straw
3. they turn a blind eye to it
4. the ideas have raised a few eyebrows
5. put yourself in their shoes
6. I've been rushed off my feet
7. the boss is breathing down my neck
8. it's a huge weight off my shoulders

8 1a. compatible 1b. compatible 2a. shrank 2b. shrinking 3a. crack 3b. Cracks 4a. fuzzy 4b. fuzzy 5a. ripped 5b. ripped 6a. falling apart 6b. fell apart 7a. frayed 7b. fray 8a. chipped 8b. chipping

Writing: Letters of complaint

1 1. addition 2. attention 3. concerning 4. unaware 5. cite 6. Surely 7. speaking 8. alternative

2 1. of the fact that 2. of 3. of the fact that 4. of the fact that 5. of 6. of
1. c. 2. f. 3. b. 4. a. 5. d. 6. e.

11 Relationships

1 1. fell out, made up 2. rub (each other) up 3. pick on 4. showing off 5. brought up 6. get away with 7. get through to

2 1. falling-out 2. get-together 3. show-off 4. dropout 5. send-off 6. breakup 7. hang-ups 8. come-on

3 1. must 2. can't 3. might 4. can't 5. have been doing 6. be feeling 7. might have 8. can't have seen

4 1. complete and utter waste, complete and utter lack 2. complete and utter failure 3. complete and utter disregard 4. complete and utter disgrace 5. complete and

utter mess   6. complete and utter breakdown
7. complete and utter bore

5 a. Suppose he was having an affair, what would you do then?
b. What's that supposed to mean?
c. How was I supposed to know?
d. They're OK I suppose, but they're not my favourite band.
e. I'm supposed to be going out, but I could get out of it.
f. It's supposed to be brilliant.
g. I was supposed to meet him last week, but he cancelled.
h. I don't suppose you could give me a lift, could you?
i. I suppose so.
1. What's that supposed to mean?
2. I'm supposed to be going out, but I could get out of it.
3. It's supposed to be brilliant.
4. Suppose he was having an affair, what would you do then?
5. how was I supposed to know?
6. I don't suppose you could give me a lift, could you?
I suppose so.

6 1. b. 2. d. 3. a. 4. c. 5. h. 6. g. 7. k. 8. i. 9. l. 10. e.
11. j. 12. f.

7 1. I wish he'd clear up once in a while.
2. All he does is sit on his backside all day playing/and play on his PlayStation.
3. He's always eavesdropping on my conversations.
4. I wish he wouldn't take the mickey out of my English all the time.
5. I wish he'd knock before barging into my room.
6. He isn't exactly the most considerate man/person I've ever met.
7. He's constantly leaving his things lying around.
8. He doesn't exactly go out of his way to be helpful.

8 1. stiff + fear   2. devastated + broke down
3. embarrassed + went   4. pissed off + bugged
5. mortified + swallow   6. collected + unflappable
7. livid + rage   8. lost + tongue-tied

9 1. we had a bit of a heart to heart   2. I managed to win them over   3. Don't take this the wrong way   4. the doctor confirmed my worst fears   5. he just went on and on about it   6. it is like talking to a brick wall   7. she was having none of it

10 1. wasn't/isn't exactly Shakespeare   2. haven't exactly set
3. isn't exactly my idea of a night out   4. aren't exactly the safest driver in the world

11 1. On the condition …   2. Assuming (that) everyone agrees …   3. Provided/Providing (that) his work …
4. … the wage demands assuming (that) the union accepts …
5. b.   6. c.   7. a.   8. d.
9. These books are lent to students on the condition that they return them within three days.
10. The competition should raise £1,000 assuming (that) everyone donates at least £50.
11. The meeting should finish at 2.45 provided that people arrive at 1.30.
12. Parcels will arrive in time for Christmas providing (that) people post them/they are posted before 10th December.

12 Economics and finance

1 1. collapsed, colossal   2. booming, tiger   3. miracle, recession   4. bottoming out   5. mess, turnaround   6. rock, picked up   7. bust   8. reforms, foundations   9. peaked, slowdown   10. wall, rocketed

2 1. economics   2. economise   3. economists
4. economically   5. economical   6. uneconomic
7. economic

3 1. fan/supporter   2. stand   3. favour   4. theory
5. opposed   6. minds   7. support   8. doubts

4 1. drastic   2. tight   3. crippling   4. dismal   5. grave
6. draconian   7. dwindling   8. bright

5 1. set   2. out   3. from   4. for   5. losses   6. breaking
7. stock   8. price   9. burst   10. takeover   11. against
12. recommended

6 1. the worst of all worlds, I would have been better off
2. difficult at the best of times   3. things have taken a turn for the worse   4. we'll just have to make the best of a bad job   5. I spent the best part of ten years   6. it's better than a kick in the teeth   7. things have definitely changed for the better   8. if the worst comes to the worst

7 1. burden, write off, incur   2. crippling, stand, settle
3. got into, ran up, cleared, restructure, collector, outstanding

Writing: Anecdotes

1 1. worse   2. eavesdropping   3. blame   4. due   5. burst
6. happen   7. about   8. finally   9. direction   10. straight
11. fate

2 1. peered   2. whispering   3. hobble   4. smashed
5. giggling   6. trudge   7. leering   8. was (just) gazing
9. strut   10. mumbled   11. sprinted   12. screeched

Grammar: The future

1 1. I've got to   2. should   3. be lounging   4. I'll be seeing, I'll let   5. supposed to be going   6. just about to, I'll   7. going to have to   8. bound to find out   9. on the verge of becoming   10. coming down

2 1. leaves, are (you) flying   2. 'm/am going to be sick   3. are (you) doing, was going to meet   4. 'm/am going to try
5. finish/'ve/have finished, 'll/will have paid back   6. won't tell

3 1. The takeover seems quite unlikely to be approved.
2. BT are set to announce record profits today.
3. The firm is to be taken over.
4. The whole village is on the point of being swallowed up by the sea.
5. Tigers are now on the verge of extinction in many parts of the country.

13 Books, films and music

1 1. one-dimensional, relate, developed   2. classics, in translation   3. sitting, page-turner   4. heavy-going, chapters
5. rhyme   6. moving, soppy   7. gory, scene   8. genre, cross
9. hyped-up, let-down   10. convoluted, preposterous

2 1. mainstream, underground   2. catchy   3. cover, original
4. remix   5. sampled, rapped   6. solos

3 1. hurt   2. say   3. let go   4. tell   5. happen   6. speak
7. let it lie   8. admit   9. repeat   10. get into
a. – 3., 4., 6., 7., 8., 9.   b. – 1., 10.   c. – 2., 5.

4 1. would've/would have, hadn't had to work
2. would've/would have, 'd/had been   3. would, wasn't/weren't   4. would've/would have, hadn't kept
5. would, wasn't/weren't working   6. 'd/would go out, had

5 1. 'll/will do yourself   2. have shot themselves   3. excusing myself   4. prides itself   5. topping themselves, throw themselves   6. beating yourself up/beating yourselves up   7. hurting yourself/yourselves

6 1. drummer   2. saxophonist   3. immigrant   4. labourer   5. academic   6. traffickers   7. criminal   8. hypocrite   9. surgeon

7 1. to   2. going   3. from   4. mood   5. out   6. toying   7. of/about   8. fancy   9. way   10. for   11. does   12. into   13. on   14. lift   15. arm   16. make   17. safe   18. dot

8 2. you went <u>to</u> with   3. telling you <u>about</u> the other day   4. I applied <u>for</u>   5. I play <u>for</u> on Sundays   6. I'd think <u>of</u> for a night out   7. you referred <u>to</u> in your lecture   8. the last film he was <u>in</u>, which I can't remember the name <u>of</u> now   9. I'm absolutely useless <u>at</u> by the way, I study Spanish <u>with</u>

9 1. Thorny, a long-running   2. fairly, hard   3. Cover   4. premium, renewed   5. A veteran, futuristic

10 1. Regrettably   2. Basically   3. Interestingly   4. Admittedly   5. Understandably   6. Hopefully   7. Worryingly   8. Remarkably   9. Regrettably   10. Remarkably   11. Worryingly   12. Luckily   13. Unsurprisingly   14. Basically

14 War and peace

1 1. step up   2. prop up   3. bring about   4. drum up   5. pull out   6. intervene   7. hack   8. twist   9. distract   10. fuel

2 1. dictatorship, dictatorial   2. precision, precisely   3. intervention, intervening   4. grievances, grievous   5. liberators, liberation   6. invasion, invaders   7. unprovoked, provocation   8. fanatical, fanatics/fanaticism

3 1. bled   2. natural causes   3. choked   4. childbirth, broken heart   5. driven   6. crushed   7. starved   8. dragged

4 1. break   2. impartial   3. gung-ho   4. demented   5. brainwashed   6. censorship   7. get rid of   8. stick

5 1. casualties   2. reparations   3. crimes, hero   4. veterans   5. brink

6 1. overthrow, install   2. conducted, forcing   3. dispute   4. annulled, outlawed

7 a. 5.   b. 3.   c. 7.   d. 6.   e. 1.   f. 8.   g. 2.   h. 4.

8 1. b.   2. a.   3. e.   4. d.   5. c.

9 1. War   2. warring   3. battle, war   4. battles   5. war   6. battle   7. war   8. battle   9. war   10. battle

Writing: Using visual information

1 1. proposals   2. graph   3. bar   4. apart   5. rate   6. steeply   7. proportion   8. little   9. slightly   10. surprisingly   11. gained   12. favour

2 1. forward   2. into   3. in   4. between   5. from   6. for

3 1. steeply   2. clearly   3. gained   4. support   5. rate   6. staggering

15 Ceremonies, celebrations and culture

1 1. best man, bridesmaids   2. civil, registry office   3. vows   4. wedding list   5. silver   6. aisle   7. cremated, scattered   8. coffin, tears   9. grave, buried   10. condolences   11. urn, shrine

2 1. c.   2. h.   3. g.   4. a.   5. e.   6. b.   7. f.   8. d.

3 1. tears   2. cry   3. crying   4. tear   5. sobbing, floods

4 1. the rich, the poor   2. the dead   3. the homeless   4. the elderly   5. the unemployed   6. the needy   7. the living

5 1. wear whatever I want at work   2. however long it takes   3. wherever my boss sends me   4. Whoever told you that   5. Whenever/Whatever time of day I've tried to phone   6. whatever it

6 1. laid, played, released   2. attended, entertained, washed down   3. awards, do, dignitaries   4. symbolising, cheering, watching   a. – 4.   b. – 3.   c. – 2.   d. – 1.

7 2. considering how ill I felt   3. considering how young he is   4. considering how dangerous the situation was   5. considering how few resources they have   6. considering how long it has taken so far   7. considering how many players were missing

8 1. hyper   2. pro   3. over   4. post   5. pre   6. anti   7. under   8. counter   9. semi   10. sub   a. (over)indulged   b. (under)estimated   c. (pre)paid   d. (pro-)life   e. (hyper)active   f. (counter-)productive   g. (post-)natal, (anti-)depressants   h. (sub)consciously

9 1. unlike   2. whereas   3. whereas   4. unlike   5. Unlike   6. compared   7. opposed   8. contrast   9. contrasted   10. comparison   11. There is a lot of violence in films today compared to thirty years ago.   12. The English eat dinner early, unlike the Spanish, who eat much later.   13. A large number of children spend much of their free time on the computer, as opposed to ten years ago, when they did sport.   14. There are no restrictions on the days lorry drivers can drive in Britain whereas in France they can't drive on Sundays.

16 Health and medicine

1 1. lame   2. unhealthy   3. fatal   4. bruised   5. infectious   6. sick   7. healthy   8. crippled   9. wounds   10. scars   11. symptom   12. wounds   13. ills   14. pain   15. cancer   16. headache

2 1. diagnosis   2. untreatable   3. vaccination   4. supplementary   5. paralysis   6. repetitive   7. traumatised   8. infestation

3 1. run-up   2. golden   3. last   4. eleventh   5. halfway   6. height   7. wake   8. nick

4 1. suffers   2. causing   3. lead   4. diet   5. number/series   6. operation   7. raise   8. met   9. way   10. opposition/resistance   11. life   12. slope

5 1. lost, battle   2. territory   3. fighting   4. minefield   5. defence, fight off   6. attack

6 1. 'll be going   2. 'll have had, 'll be looking   3. 'll have remembered, 'll have left   4. 'll be slaving, 'll be thinking   5. 'll have finished, 'll be passing, 'll have done

Writing: Reviews

1 1. justice 2. screen 3. concerned 4. scope 5. array 6. accomplished 7. treated 8. weight 9. manuscript 10. merges

2 1. b. 2. a. 3. f. 4. d. 5. c. 6. e. 7. stand-up comedy 8. diverse backgrounds 9. compulsive viewing 10. vast array 11. thoroughly recommend 12. mixed reactions

3 1. whose 2. who 3. which 4. who 5. whom 6. whose

Grammar: Suggesting and recommending

1 1. Have you tried doing 2. could try 3. Have you tried, haven't, 'll/should give 4. were, d'/would wait, could try 5. should do, were, 'd/would just give

2 1. suggest 2. advised 3. advice 4. advice, advised 5. suggested 6. suggestion 7. advice 8. suggestions/advice

3 1. should/could 2. ought, heard, try/go 3. Any, must, got 4. like, worth 5. much, miss, tip/advice 6. into, tea, consider 7. must, 'll/will

4 1. rejected 2. implement 3. strongly 4. came up with 5. highly

17 Humour

1 1. fell 2. off 3. played 4. funny 5. cracks 6. butt 7. takes 8. take 9. tease 10. laugh 11. expense 12. straight

2 1. f. 2. c. 3. a. 4. e. 5. d. 6. b. 7. k. 8. g. 9. l. 10. h. 11. i. 12. j.

3 1. self-reliant 2. self-disciplined 3. self-indulgent 4. self-righteous 5. self-important 6. self-conscious 7. self-pitying 8. self-centred

4 1. It's no laughing matter.
2. He tried to laugh it off, but I could see he was really upset about it.
3. They must be laughing all the way to the bank.
4. He's become a complete laughing stock.
5. I only did it for a laugh.
6. It was a laughable offer.
7. I nearly laughed my head off.
8. We had the last laugh.
9. You'll soon be laughing on the other side of your face.
10. You've got to laugh.
a. You'll soon be laughing on the other side of your face.
b. They must be laughing all the way to the bank.
c. He's become a complete laughing stock.
d. We had the last laugh.
e. It's no laughing matter.

5 1. laugh 2. hysterics/stitches 3. stitches/hysterics 4. tears 5. wet 6. giggle 7. giggles 8. snigger 9. chuckle 10. cackle 11. howl/roar 12. roar/howl

6 1. satirical + critique 2. dry + deadpan 3. mickey + sarcastic 4. punning + witty 5. irreverent + go 6. physical + slapstick 7. corny + sexist 8. mimic + impersonation

7 1. shouldn't have laughed 2. should've/should have brought, should see 3. should go, should be, shouldn't take 4. shouldn't have laughed/shouldn't laugh 5. shouldn't be sitting, should be studying, shouldn't worry 6. should think

8 1. j. 2. c. 3. f. 4. g. 5. d. 6. a. 7. b. 8. i. 9. h. 10. e.

9 1. f. 2. d. 3. h. 4. g. 5. a. 6. c. 7. b. 8. e.

10 1. Furthermore 2. addition 3. Not only, also 4. additional 5. further
6. Not only did she steal money from the company, but she (also) lied about her qualifications.
7. Not only has he been banned from driving for a year, but he (also) had to pay a £2,000 fine.
8. Not only should we think carefully about the cost of the project, but (also) about the environmental impact it will have.
9. Not only is the government failing to reform the education system, but it's (also) failing to deal with the crisis in the health service.
10. Not only is there a shortage of affordable housing in the area, but the population is (also) set to grow by 5 per cent.
11. Not only has he consistently created great music, but his whole lifestyle has (also) been the envy of young men the whole world over.
12. Not only is it in the EU's economic interest to act, but it is (also) their moral duty.

18 Crime

1 1. c. 2. i. 3. g. 4. a. 5. f. 6. d. 7. e. 8. l. 9. j. 10. k. 11. h. 12 b.

2 1. has been (formally) charged 2. is claimed 3. had/has hidden 4. escaped 5. held up 6. was forced 7. was treated 8. have described 9. call 10. were smashed 11. was sprayed

3 1. middle 2. bet 3. having 4. on 5. off 6. flying 7. whole 8. floods 9. over 10. least

4 1. with 2. to, by 3. of 4. of 5. without 6. in, without 7. to 8. on 9. of 10. from

5 1. c. 2. j. 3. d. 4. e. 5. i. 6. h. 7. f. 8. k. 9. b. 10. g. 11. l. 12. a.

6 1. custodial 2. imprisonment 3. decriminalise 4. conviction 5. inaccuracies 6. repeatedly 7. allegedly 8. criminally

7 1. slit + dismember 2. hit + knocked over 3. set up + transfer 4. kicked in + slash 5. comes out + laugh 6. hack + alter

Writing: Giving instructions and advice

1 1. load 2. through 3. sure 4. packed 5. treat 6. By 7. get 8. whatever 9. some 10. think 11. be 12. though 13. comes 14. time

2 1. remind 2. I wouldn't recommend 3. Don't worry about 4. make sure 5. Don't, whatever you do 6. Be warned 7. you're best 8. could you possibly

3 1. now I come to think of it 2. while I'm on the subject 3. incidentally 4. by the way 5. just before I forget 6. which reminds me

19 Sport and fitness

1 1. processed, scratch, moderation, vice 2. hypochondriac, symptoms, complaint, check-up 3. fanatic, six-pack, sit-ups, shape, dominates

2 1. k. 2. h. 3. b. 4. g. 5. a. 6. j. 7. i. 8. d. 9. c. 10. e.
11. l. 12. f.

3 1. cramps, stiff, overdo 2. pulled, agony, crutches 3. tore,
operated, recover 4. knackered, dog, burn 5. rough,
overdid, death 6. under, wrapped, love 7. down,
chucked, over 8. down, chest, round

4 1. net 2. bar 3. keeper 4. post 5. corner flag
6. penalty spot 7. penalty area 8. goal-line 9. shin pad
10. laces 11. touchline 12. studs

5 1. studs 2. keeper 3. laces 4. penalty area 5. bar
6. post 7. net 8. touchline

6 1. pathetic 2. cutthroat 3. universal 4. foul
5. mind-numbing 6. salutary 7. malign 8. civic
9. unprecedented

7 1. sights 2. shot 3. sailed 4. court 5. towel 6. horse
7. game 8. fish, sea

8 1. deck 2. clubs 3. jack 4. ace 5. shuffles 6. cut
7. deal 8. hand 9. trumps 10. chest 11. lay 12. bluff

9 1. c. 2. d. 3. a. 4. h. 5. b. 6. g. 7. e. 8. f.

10 1. e. 2. a. 3. b. 4. d. 5. c. 6. h. 7. g. 8. f. 9. i.
10. despite/notwithstanding 11. nevertheless/nonetheless
12. although/though 13. even though 14. Despite/In
spite of

20 Belief

1 1. disciplinarian 2. cynic 3. optimist 4. agnostic
5. nationalist 6. perfectionist 7. fatalist 8. realist
9. fanatic 10. atheist 11. pessimist 12. patriot

2 1. c. 2. g. 3. a. 4. f. 5. b. 6. d. 7. h. 8. e.
9. chopping and changing 10. kicking and screaming
11. ranted and raved 12. forgive and forget 13. give and
take 14. wait and see 15. pick and choose 16. mixing
and matching

3 **Places:** chapel, convent, mosque, shrine, synagogue, temple
Clothes/Objects: dog collar, incense burner, rosary beads,
skull cap, turban
People: imam, minister, priest, rabbi, vicar

4 1. worshippers 2. congregation, sermon
3. confession, mass 4. mat, Mecca 5. leaf, tiling 6. spires,
carvings

5 1. shake/undermine, reaffirms/reinforces 2. blind
3. mistaken 4. fostered/encouraged/strengthened
5. hung/clung 6. leap

Writing: Letters of request

1 1. behalf 2. understand 3. wondering 4. possible
5. appreciative 6. aware 7. kind 8. pleased 9. mutually
10. question

2 1. Would it be at all possible to 2. Would you be so kind
as to 3. I would be most grateful if you could possibly
4. I would greatly appreciate it if you could 5. I was
wondering if you would be kind enough to 6. I am afraid I
would not be able to

3 1. favour 2. wondering, way/possibility 3. happen, about,
would 4. suppose, could, 'd/would, grateful

Grammar: Past tenses referring to different times

1 1. present/future 2. past 3. past 4. present/future
5. present/future 6. present/future 7. past
8. present/future 9. present/future 10. present/future
11. present/future 12. present/future 13. past
14. present/future
a. – 6., 9. b. – 4., 10., 12. c. 1., 5., 11. d. – 8., 14.

2 1. didn't realise, wonder, did 2. was (vaguely) thinking, had,
were, do, ask, introduced 3. left, didn't, 'm/am (always)
going, wasn't/weren't, have, don't get 4. stopped, started,
means, risk, were

21 Travel and tourism

1 1. straight 2. crashing 3. cut 4. swerve 5. ran out
6. clipped 7. windscreen 8. dodge 9. opened
10. skidding

2 1. g. 2. e. 3. i. 4. a. 5. j. 6. c. 7. d. 8. f. 9. h. 10. b.

3 1. goose 2. dogs 3. bird 4. camel's 5. horse's
6. donkey's 7. Cat 8. dogs

4 1. believe 2. accept 3. listen 4. leave 5. download
6. heal 7. budge

5 1. the blind leading the blind 2. blind obedience
3. blindingly obvious 4. in my blind spot 5. swears blind
6. blind us with science 7. turn a blind eye to it 8. do it
blindfold 9. blind drunk 10. in blind panic
a. swears blind b. in my blind spot c. blind us with science
d. in blind panic e. the blind leading the blind f. blindingly
obvious g. do it blindfold h. blind drunk i. blind
obedience j. turn a blind eye to it

6 1. ignorance 2. boredom 3. frustration 4. desperation
5. gratitude 6. curiosity 7. loyalty

7 1. g. 2. i. 3. e. 4. a. 5. h. 6. j. 7. d. 8. b. 9. f. 10. c.
a. exceed (the) speed (limit) b. (the turning's) coming up
c. (a) hairpin/sharp (bend) d. (it's) his right of (way)
e. (replace a) burst (water) main f. (go) the long (way)
round

8 1. ventured 2. hitting 3. tomorrow 4. let 5. Wish
6. trekking 7. track 8. accompanied 9. rafting
10. highlight 11. lifetime 12. jetting 13. fund 14. hanging
out 15. pick up 16. settled in

9 1. factor 2. led 3. rise 4. triggered 5. role 6. down
7. influenced 8. brought 9. stems 10. hand 11. from
12. to 13. about 14. to 15. in

22 Youth and experience

1 1. sweet 2. encouraging 3. teething 4. puerile 5. out of
control, snigger 6. cheeky 7. rebellious 8. crawl
9. supportive 10. over-protective 11. earnest

2 2. My granddad and his friends 'll/will spend hours
reminiscing about the good old days.
3. Even when it's freezing cold, he'll walk around wearing a
T-shirt.
4. Most nights, he'll/he will pig out at McDonald's and leave
(all) the wrappers lying around.
5. He'll/will sometimes tell me his brain won't stop going
round and round.
6. What we'll/we will usually do at/over Christmas is
(we'll/we will) have a big family get-together.

7. Sometimes what she'll/she will do is a whole jigsaw puzzle – upside down!

8. She's still pretty sprightly, but she won't usually walk more than a few hundred metres.

9. He won't normally do what I tell him unless I give him a little snack as a reward.

3 1. forward 2. even 3. themselves 4. payments 5. one
6. facing 7. according 8. to 9. matters
10. circumstances/situations 11. first 12. fact 13. level
14. on 15. account 16. all 17. what
18. existing/present/current

4 1. d. 2. g. 3. i. 4. a. 5. b. 6. j. 7. f. 8. c. 9. h. 10. e.

5 2. There's no need to heat the milk
3. There's no point (in) trying to talk to them.
4. It's no good crying.
5. there's no sign (that) things are improving/will improve.
6. There's really no excuse for behaving that way
7. They were left with no choice but to sack him
8. (it's) no wonder they're in debt!

6 1. buggy 2. dummy 3. beaker 4.. pram 5. cot 6. bib
7. playpen 8. rattle

Writing: Reports

1 1. findings 2. consisted 3. range 4. Overall 5. general
6. commented 7. Regarding 8. ran 9. attitude
10. introduce 11. consider

2 1. is based on, was conducted 2. was questioned 3. were raised, are outlined 4. were/are rated, were singled out
5. were made, to have been implemented

3 1. indicated 2. pointed out 3. commented on 4. voiced concerns 5. praised 6. expressed a desire

23 Taboos and embarrassing situations

1 1. nerve 2. ice 3. foot 4. no-no 5. stick
6. taboo/sensitive, stay/steer 7. disaster/hazard 8. tongue

2 1. (mis)perception 2. view 3. realisation
4. marginalisation 5. blasphemy 6. infiltration

3 1. god-awful 2. God's gift to women 3. God knows
4. godsend 5. God-given 6. godforsaken 7. hope to God 8. My God 9. the fear of God 10. God forbid
11. play God 12. in God's name

4 2. No sooner had the question left my lips than I realised I'd really put my foot in it!
3. No sooner had I finished writing this letter to her than the phone rang and it was her!
4. No sooner had Wigan equalised than Arsenal went up the other end and scored the winner!
5. No sooner had the lift stopped than the lights went out and we were left in total darkness.
6. No sooner had we finished putting the tent up than it started raining.
7. No sooner had I plugged in the webcam than it started playing up.

5 1. tirade 2. fiasco 3. doppelganger 4. aficionado
5. stampede 6. embargo 7. zeitgeist 8. bravado

6 1. RSVP 2. MP 3. PC 4. ASAP 5. IMF 6. NB
7. NGO 8. MRSA 9. CIA 10. NATO

7 1. chill 2. cold 3. heated, boiled over, cool off 4. warm, cold 5. frosty, warmed

8 1. change 2. grip 3. majority 4. abuse 5. tolerance
6. curse 7. tradition

9 1. c. 2. d. 3. e. 4. a. 5. b.

10 1. e. 2. a. 3. b. 4. c. 5. d.
6. knock-on effect 7. As a result 8. Consequently
9. resulting in 10. Therefore

24 Celebrity and scandal

1 1. former, embroiled, doing 2. lucrative, stint, launched
3. shot, consecutive, rough 4. hits, pear-shaped, wrangling
5. host, contestants, stir 6. chequered, maverick, lay

2 1. revived 2. carve out 3. ruined 4. embarked
5. spanning 6. has been dogged 7. take off 8. launched
9. ups, downs 10. prospects 11. peak 12. structure
13. guidance

3 1. correct 2. incorrect 3. correct 4. incorrect
5. incorrect 6. incorrect 7. correct 8. correct
9. correct 10. incorrect 11. incorrect 12. correct
a. straight and narrow b. all or nothing c. ins and outs
d. make or break e. sink or swim f. to and fro g. give or take h. sooner or later

4 1. split 2. weds 3. axed 4. Dumped 5. foiled 6. sham
7. haul 8. blaze 9. probe 10. quizzed

5 1. d. 2. a. 3. c. 4. b. 5. g. 6. f. 7. h. 8. e.

6 1. endemic 2. shooting up 3. snort 4. habit
5. prescription 6. care 7. draconian 8. rehab 9. relapse

Writing: Presentations

1 1. bore 2. comprehensive 3. tight 4. position 5. briefly
6. handout 7. contrast 8. point 9. aware 10. expect
11. forgot 12. reminds

2 1. utilise 2. relocate 3. amalgamate 4. remunerate
5. consolidate 6. accelerate 7. formulate 8. penetrate
9. calculate 10. collaborate on 11. exploit 12. capitalise on

3 1. Everybody knows that the English will bet on almost anything!
2. A lot of people don't realise that 80 per cent of the world's millionaires are self-employed.
3. They've shown that in countries where drugs are legal, use drops significantly.
4. They're suggesting that the price war is a consequence of globalisation.
5. Almost everyone agrees that the rich liver longer.

Using Grammar: Conditionals

1 1. If only 2. assuming 3. provided 4. suppose
5. whether 6. so long 7. even if 8. had 9. unless
10. Should

2 1. c. 2. g. 3. j. 4. e. 5. i. 6. b. 7. a. 8. f. 9. h. 10. d.
11. get, go, 'll/will love 12. get, will get 13. couldn't stop, tried 14. 'd/had been, have been/be 15. 'll/will give, like